Communications in Computer and Information Science   1683

More information about this series at https://link.springer.com/bookseries/7899

Luis Bathen · Gokay Saldamli · Xiaoyan Sun ·
Thomas H. Austin · Alex J. Nelson (Eds.)

Silicon Valley Cybersecurity Conference

Third Conference, SVCC 2022
Virtual Event, August 17–19, 2022
Revised Selected Papers

 Springer

Editors
Luis Bathen
IBM Research
San Jose, CA, USA

Gokay Saldamli
San José State University
San Jose, CA, USA

Xiaoyan Sun
California State University
Sacramento, CA, USA

Thomas H. Austin
San Jose State University
San Jose, CA, USA

Alex J. Nelson
National Institute of Standards
and Technology
Gaithersburg, MD, USA

ISSN 1865-0929   ISSN 1865-0937 (electronic)
Communications in Computer and Information Science
ISBN 978-3-031-24048-5   ISBN 978-3-031-24049-2 (eBook)
https://doi.org/10.1007/978-3-031-24049-2

Preface

The Silicon Valley Cybersecurity Conference (SVCC) is an annual international conference in cybersecurity held at the heart of Silicon Valley, which is supported by the Silicon Valley Cybersecurity Institute (SVCSI). SVCC focuses on research in dependability, reliability, and security to address cyber-attacks, vulnerabilities, faults, and errors in networks and systems. This conference is a forum to present research in robustness and resilience in a wide spectrum of computing systems and networks. All aspects of the research and practice of applied security are within the scope of this conference. Relevant topics include innovative system design, protocols, and algorithms for detecting, preventing, mitigating, and responding to malicious threats in dependable and secure systems and networks including experimentation and assessment. The topics of interest include the security of hardware, software, networks, clouds, cyber-physical systems, socio-technical systems, blockchain, and healthcare.

In 2022, SVCC had three keynote speakers and also featured a CyberWarrior cybersecurity competition. The conference accepted seven papers out of ten submitted. Papers were evaluated with a double blind review process, with three reviews per paper.

In 2022, the conference was supported by Google, Cisco, and The Select Group.

August 2022

Luis Bathen
Gokay Saldamli
Xiaoyan Sun

Organization

General Chairs

Divyesh Jadav   IBM Research, USA
Younghee Park   San Jose State University, USA

Program Chairs

Luis Bathen   IBM Research, USA
Gokay Saldamli   San Jose State University, USA
Xiaoyan Sun   California State University, Sacramento, USA

Publicity Chairs

Sara Tehranipoor   Santa Clara University, USA
Wei Yan   Chinese Academy of Sciences, China

Publication Chairs

Thomas H. Austin   San Jose State University, USA
Alex J. Nelson   National Institute of Standards and Technology,
                           USA

Registration Chairs

Fabio Di Troia   San Jose State University, USA
Khanh Nguyen   San Jose State University, USA

Poster Chairs

Nima Karimian   San Jose State University, USA
Hyoungshick Kim   Sungkyunkwan University, South Korea

Special Session Chairs

Jinoh Kim   Texas A&M University, Commerce, USA
Ikkyun Kim   Electronics and Telecommunications Research
                           Institute, South Korea

Hackathon Chairs

Sang-Yoon Chang   University of Colorado, Colorado Springs, USA
Jackie Zhang   Fort Hays State University, USA
Michael Wang   Vitapoly Inc., USA

Technical Program Committee

Vikrant Nanda   Google Inc., USA
Subhash Lakshminarayana   University of Warwick, UK
Malek Ben Salem   Accenture Inc., USA
Sang Kil Cha   Korea Advanced Institute of Science and
     Technology, South Korea
Harshan Jagadeesh   Indian Institute of Technology Delhi, India
Chang-Wu Chen   imToken, Taiwan
Carlos Rubio-Medrano   Texas A&M University Corpus Christi, USA
Eul Gyu Im   Hanyang University, South Korea
Lei Xu   University of Texas Rio Grande Valley, USA
Xiaoyan (Sherry) Sun   California State University, Sacramento, USA
Tai M. Chung   Sungkyunkwan University, South Korea
Liudong Xing   University of Massachusetts Dartmouth, USA
Sangwon Hyun   Myongji University, South Korea
Daisuke Mashima   Illinois at Singapore Pte Ltd, Singapore
Sung Lee   VMWare, USA
Sandra Céspedes   University of Chile, Chile
Mohammadreza   University of Potsdam, Germany
Ashouri Francesco Mercaldo   Università degli Studi del Molise, Italy
Carlos Rubio-Medrano   Arizona State University, USA
Wenjun Fan   University of Colorado, Colorado Springs, USA
Ihor Vasyltsov   Samsung Electronics, South Korea
Wei Yan   Clarkson University, USA
Ahyoung Lee   Kennesaw State University, USA
Daisuke Mashima   Advanced Digital Sciences Center, Singapore
Thomas H. Austin   San Jose State University, USA
Hsiang-Jen Hong   University of Colorado, Colorado Springs, USA
Hossein Sayadi   California State University, Long Beach, USA
Hyoungshick Kim   Sungkyunkwan University, South Korea
Attila Altay Yavuz   University of South Florida, USA
Donghyun (David) Kim   Georgia State University, USA
Jinoh Kim   Texas A&M University, Commerce, USA
Hongxin Hu   Clemson University, USA
Jorjeta Jetcheva   San Jose State University, USA
Tamzidul Hoque   University of Kansas, USA

Arman Roohi	University of Nebraska at Lincoln, USA
Paul Wortman	University of Connecticut, USA
Samah Saeed	The City College of New York, USA
Sara Tehranipoor	Santa Clara University, USA
Prabha Sundaravadivel	The University of Texas at Tyler, USA
Samaneh Ghandali	Google, USA
Nima Karimian	San Jose State University, USA
Kohei Shiomoto	Tokyo City University, Japan
Qiong Zhang	Fujitsu Lab, USA
Mohammad Husain	California State Polytechnic University, USA
Daehee Seo	Sangmyung University, South Korea
Zhang Tianwei	Nanyang Technological University, Singapore
Gokay Saldamli	San Jose State University, USA
YoungHyun Oh	IBM, USA
T. J. O'Connor	Florida Institute of Technology, USA

Webmasters

Monil Sakhidas	San Jose State University, USA
Khan Nguyen	San Jose State University, USA

Contents

Contents

Malware Analysis

Robustness of Image-Based Malware Analysis

Katrina Tran, Fabio Di Troia, and Mark Stamp(✉)

San Jose State University, San Jose, USA
mark.stamp@sjsu.edu

Abstract. In previous work, "gist descriptor" features extracted from images have been used in malware classification problems and have shown promising results. In this research, we determine whether gist descriptors are robust with respect to malware obfuscation techniques, as compared to Convolutional Neural Networks (CNN) trained directly on malware images. Using the Python Image Library (PIL), we create images from malware executables and from malware that we obfuscate. We conduct experiments to compare classifying these images with a CNN as opposed to extracting the gist descriptor features from these images to use in classification. For the gist descriptors, we consider a variety of classification algorithms including k-nearest neighbors, random forest, support vector machine, and multi-layer perceptron. We find that gist descriptors are more robust than CNNs, with respect to the obfuscation techniques that we consider.

Keywords: Malware · Convolutional neural network · Gist descriptors

1 Introduction

Malware is software created with the intent to be malicious or have a malicious effect [1]. Malware includes threats like viruses, worms, Trojan horses, and spyware. It can even be used in connection with other kinds of security threats like spam, bugs, and denial-of-service attacks. As a result of these factors, many people fall into the trap of having their devices infected with malware. In 2019, Kaspersky Lab released a threat report that stated that the number of users who encountered malware had tripled to 1.7 million [12].

Due to the recent COVID-19 pandemic, there has been an increase in people spending time online. An empirical study of the relation of cybercrime and COVID-19 found that there was a positive relationship between the number of malware infections with closed non-essential businesses and the number of malware infections with positive COVID-19 cases [4]. In this time period, people have to stay at home and interact with others online. This causes an increase in online presence. The more people there are online, the more people there are to fall victim to malware attacks. In addition to this, malware is constantly evolving to bypass security measures that protect devices. The attackers that create the

L. Bathen et al. (Eds.): SVCC 2022, CCIS 1683, pp. 3–21, 2022.
https://doi.org/10.1007/978-3-031-24049-2_1

malware can even use obfuscation techniques to disguise the malware to prevent it from being detected.

Image-based malware analysis is the study of malware converted to images to identify them. There are many machine learning algorithms that are useful in classifying images and have helped in making this approach successful. Often when looking at image classification, Convolutional Neural Networks (CNN) are used. CNNs are fast, extracting information easily, and give high accuracies. However, with certain obfuscation techniques, CNNs cannot give the same high accuracies [14].

This makes it important to also study the results of malware obfuscation with respect to images. In the field of image-based malware analysis, one approach is the use of so-called "gist" descriptors, which are designed to extract general features from images [13]. Using gist descriptors might reduce the effectiveness of some types of obfuscation that are commonly applied to malware. In previous research the robustness of gist descriptors in the malware domain was briefly considered [13].

In this paper, the main objective is to extensively analyze the robustness of gist descriptors as features for malware classification. With the gist descriptors as features, we use four different classifiers to compare to the accuracy that a deep learning algorithm, CNN, can have on an image of malware. This paper is structured in sections as follows. In Sect. 2 we review representative examples of relevant related work. Section 3 introduces a wide range of relevant background topics. Section 4 consists of the experiments done for this research and the results. Section 5 summarizes our experimental findings and discusses future work.

2   Related Work

There are several examples of research in image-based malware analysis. Most of this research is based on converting binary files to grayscale images but color images have recently been studied. There are many different ways to create such color images. In some of the related work, obfuscation was considered.

2.1   Color Images for Malware Analysis

A crucial part of image-based malware analysis is in the images that the analysis is performed on. This means that the way these images are created from the malware is important. Many different ways to create these images have been considered.

A common methods to create malware images focuses on the bytes of the executable. D. Vasan et al. [12] considered the malware files as a binary object, converted the binary to an 8-bit vector, and then organized it into a 2D array, which can be represented as a grayscale image. Applying a color-map onto the 2D array would result in a color image. In another approach, J. Fu et al. [3] manipulated the bytes in a more complicated manner. With the malware file, J. Fu et al. only focused on the bits in the PE sections because they contain the crucial information of the executable related to its structure. Since RGB images are made of three channels, the PE format section is split up again into three sections to set up for each of the channels. After the split, the entropy values, byte values, and relative size values are computed with the bytes of the binary to create RGB channels. The entropy values, byte values, and relative size values are computed because they can also be important features that reflect aspects of malware and computing them can create malware images that reflect that feature. These two methods have achieved a high accuracy of more than 90%. While the method from J. Fu et al. obtained higher accuracies, it is computationally expensive when compared to the approach by D. Vasan et al.

Another approach to creating images from malware is based on the instructions of the executable. To get the instructions of a malware executable, the file is first disassembled to obtain assembly code and mnemonic opcodes are extracted. J. Chen [2] took these instructions and filtered for the ones that would be more closely aligned with actions malware could use to do harm. These instructions are grouped together in threes and each instruction is taken as their machine code form to create the bytes for a pixel of an RGB image. In a slightly different approach, K. Han et al. [5] considered the instructions in a more complicated way. They also filtered for specific instructions but took the opcode sequences and put them through a hash to obtain an RGB color alongside the coordinates for that color to be converted in an image matrix. The images created from this approach look vastly different from the other approaches because, instead of an image with every pixel representing a part of the malware, this approach uses an image matrix and creates specific RGB pixels depending on a specific location. This means that not all the coordinates of the image are utilized. Creating images based on instructions is reasonable and allows for a more guided approach on filtering unnecessary information. However, disassembling an executable and filtering for instructions is a costly operation.

2.2 Obfuscation

Malware writer use obfuscation as a means to evade detection. There are many different approaches to malware obfuscation. To deal with malware obfuscation, various techniques that have been developed considered in the malware analysis literature.

S. Yajamanam et al. [13] used gist descriptors. From the malware images, gist descriptors are extracted to be used in classifying the malware. Gist descriptors are designed to get the "gist" of the crucial components of an image. Extracting the gist of the malware image means learning the general points of the malware, which might increase the likelihood of ignoring obfuscations. In another approach, H. Yakura et al. [14] proposed an image creation method that extracted sequences from the whole binary data. This method makes the model overcome obfuscation techniques that would be implemented in the data section. This idea is similar to the previous method of dealing with malware obfuscation, namely, they want to look at the "big picture" so that the parts that have been obfuscated do not confuse the model from classifying the malware correctly.

3   Background

In this Section, we first introduce the various classifiers that are used in our experiments. Then, we summarize the computing environment and we provide details on the dataset. We also discuss the various methods that we used to generate images from malware samples, and we introduce the obfuscation techniques that we employ in our robustness experiments. We conclude this Section with a discussion of gist descriptors, which are an integral component of the experiments and results in Sect. 4.

3.1   Classifiers

In this research, several different classifiers were used to classify the malware. To test the robustness of gist descriptors, they were applied as features when classifying with classification algorithms k-Nearest Neighbor (k-NN), Random Forest, Support Vector Machine (SVM), and Multi-Layer Perceptron (MLP). As a comparison, a Convolutional Neural Network (CNN) was used to classify based on the images themselves.

k-Nearest Neighbor. The k-Nearest Neighbor (k-NN) approach is a supervised machine learning algorithm. It requires data from a training dataset that includes the labels. The classification of new points is based on that data. Such classification is based on a voting system. It takes a new point and classifies it based on the k-number of neighbors that are closest to that point. As shown in Fig. 1, the point x is the new point that needs to be classified. Depending on the k value chosen, k-NN calculates the k number of nearest points to x to determine if it belongs to the b-class or the r-class. For example, if k was 3, the x point looks at the three closest points to it. In this case, it is closest to two r-class data points and one b-class data point, thus, the majority rules the x point to be classified as r-class.

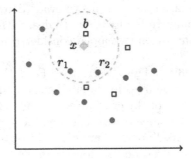

Fig. 1. k-Nearest neighbor [11]

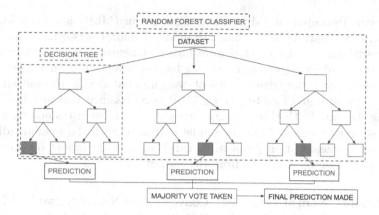

Fig. 2. Random forest [7]

Fig. 3. Support vector machine [11]

Random Forest. Random Forest is a classification algorithm based on decision trees. A decision tree takes a dataset and splits it into branches based on different decisions that it makes about the features. This algorithm creates multiple decision trees as shown in Fig. 2, showing different possibilities of decision trees that can be created from the dataset. The data point that has to be classified is in these multiple decision trees. Its classification, then, depends on the majority prediction that is made from the multiple decision trees.

Support Vector Machine. Support Vector Machine (SVM) is a supervised machine learning algorithm. Based on a training dataset, the algorithm decides on a hyperplane that best separates the classes from each other. As shown in Fig. 3, the red-class data points and blue-class data points are separated by the yellow hyperplane. The classification of new points depends on which side of the hyperplane they lie. For this example, if it is on the upper right side of the hyperplane, it will classify as red-class.

Multi-layer Perceptron. Multi-Layer Perceptron (MLP) is a deep learning algorithm. Deep learning algorithms are made of neural networks, which are a set of algorithms that are created from layers of neurons. As shown in Fig. 4, it is comprised of an input layer, several hidden layers, and an output layer. Between each layer, the edges represent weights that decide the output node that a data point would lead to. To use MLP as a classifier, it is first trained on a training dataset. With this training dataset, the model is trained by setting and adjusting its weights. After the model is trained with the weights adjusted to the specific classification problem, it can then classify inputs by predicting what the classification would be from the output.

Convolutional Neural Network. Convolutional Neural Network (CNN) is a deep learning algorithm. Like the MLP, it is also comprised of a neural network. However, the CNN includes a convolutional layer and a pooling layer. The convolutional layer of a CNN preprocesses the image and extracts feature information from the images. It creates a convolved feature. The pooling layer then takes this convolved feature and reduces it. The structure of this neural network is different from the MLP. Like the MLP, though, it first trains on a training dataset to set its weights for the specific problem and performs classifications based on the trained model.

3.2 Computing Environment

The environment used to conduct experiments for this research is shown in Table 1. A Jupyter notebook in Python was used to perform these experiments, while a Jupyter notebook in MATLAB was used to extract the gist descriptor features from the images.

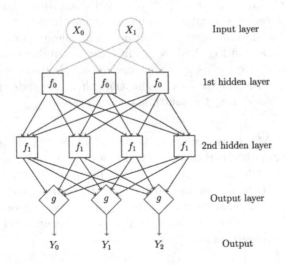

Fig. 4. Multi-layer perceptron [11]

Table 1. Computing environment

System	Description
Virtual Machine Software	Oracle VM VirtualBox
Operating System	Ubuntu 20.04.3
Base Memory	4096 MB
Number of Processors	4
Python Version	3.9.7
Python Libraries	pandas, PIL, NumPy, TensorFlow, Keras, scikit-learn, cv2
MATLAB Version	9.11
MATLAB Frameworks	Deep Learning Toolbox, Image Processing Toolbox

3.3   Dataset

This dataset was from a project called the Malicia Project [8]. The project is a collection of malware binaries that were collected from 500 drive-by download servers over 11 months. Table 2 shows information about the dataset files. Table 3 shows the malware features for each file. Table 4 shows the top five families and the number of files in each.

In the dataset, the malware binaries had to be extracted from the folders. The labels were also extracted. After extracting the labels, the data had to be cleaned and checked for missing labels. Through this process, we were able to find that there were 1,759 files that were missing a family label. There were also 305 files missing the file type label. These files were excluded from the experiments.

We also only focused on the executable files. This means that we exclusively focused on the files with the file type label "EXE." Besides the executable files, there were also 276 dynamic-link library files. These were not used. These experiments focused only on the top five largest families: Winwebsec, Zbot, Zeroaccess, Securityshield, and Cridex. In these five families, there was only one dynamic-link library file in Zbot, making the number of Zbot family files that we used equal to 2,167.

Table 2. Malicia dataset details

Description	Number
Total files	11,668
Executable	11,087
Dynamic-link library	276
Files with no extension label	305
Maximum executable size (bytes)	1,595,576
Minimum executable size (bytes)	3,677
Families	54
Families with 1 file	23
Files with no family label	1,759

Table 3. Malicia dataset features

Feature	Data Type
file ID	INT
SHA1	VARCHAR
size	INT
file type	ENUM
packer	VARCHAR
in store	TINYINT
icon	VARCHAR
icon size	INT
icon label	VARCHAR
family	VARCHAR
traffic label	VARCHAR
traffic	TINYINT
affiliate	VARCHAR
sshot label	VARCHAR

Table 4. Malicia dataset largest families

Family name	Total files
Winwebsec	5,820
Zbot	2,168
Zeroaccess	1,306
Securityshield	150
Cridex	74

3.4 Images from Malware

In our research, the Python Image Library (PIL) was used to create the images from malware executables. The PIL takes bytes from the executables and creates the images from those bytes. The size of the images created for the experiments are 60 × 60. This size was chosen because the smallest sized file we consider is 3,677 bytes. The PIL would not be able to make larger images. We wanted to keep the image size consistent and the executables were truncated to only take the number of bytes necessary for the image to be created. The PIL offers different modes for the images to be created into and these different modes are explored in the experiments [6]. Such modes represent different ways to create the images. It determines what the type and depth of a pixel for each image. The modes used in our experiments are listed in Table 5.

Table 5. Image modes tested

Mode	Size	Description
1	1-bit pixels	Black and white, one pixel per byte
L	8-bit pixels	Black and white
RGB	3 × 8-bit pixels	True color
CMYK	4 × 8-bit pixels	Color separation
YCbCr	3 × 8-bit pixels	Color video format

To perform these experiments, the images were created first. The top five largest families were all converted to images. Different image mode versions of each of the malware files were created and saved. Examples of a malware executable converted to imaged form in some of the different color modes are shown in Fig. 5.

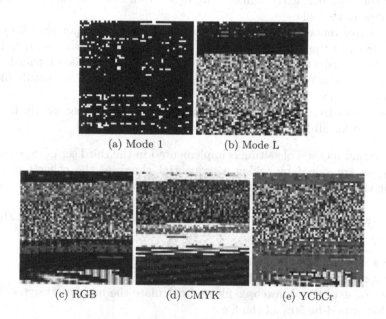

(a) Mode 1   (b) Mode L

(c) RGB   (d) CMYK   (e) YCbCr

Fig. 5. Python image library modes

3.5 Obfuscating Malware Images

The obfuscation technique we applied in this research is salting. In each family, we salted all of the files with another family in percentages. These are in pairs since the experiments are all binary classification experiments. We applied two different salting techniques in this research.

The amount of obfuscation is based on percentage of the file. Specifically, we considered 10%, 30%, 50%, 60%, 75%, 80%, and 100% for the Winwebsec versus Zbot experiments, and 10%, 50%, 75%, and 100% with the other family pairs.

The first method of salting is implemented in the second set of experiments. The images are salted by taking random bytes of the other family to salt the original family. We refer to this approach as random salting.

For example, if we are trying to salt the Winwebsec family with Zbot, we take each file in the Winwebsec family and convert a specific percentage of the file to a random section of a Zbot file.

For example, the steps of this process using Winwebsec salted by Zbot by 50% are:

1. Take a file in the Winwebsec family
2. Take a random file in the Zbot family
3. Get the size of the Winwebsec file and calculate the number of bytes of that file that would be 50% of the file
4. With that number, extract that many bytes from the Zbot family at random positions in that file
5. Those bytes replace the Winwebsec family at the same spot that they were taken from in the Zbot file (ex. if the byte at index 12 was taken from the Zbot file, replace the byte at index 12 in the Winwebsec file by that byte)
6. This results in a Winwebsec family file obfuscated by the Zbot family file and the image is saved
7. Repeat steps from the beginning with the next Winwebsec family file until performed for all files in the Winwebsec family.

The second method of salting is implemented in the third set of experiments. The images are salted by taking a sequential chunk of the other family and replacing the end of the original family file with it. We refer to this as contiguous salting.

For example, the steps of this process using Winwebsec salted by Zbot by 50% are:

1. Take a file in the Winwebsec family
2. Take a random file in the Zbot family
3. Get the size of the Winwebsec file and calculate the number of bytes of that file that would be 50% of the file
4. With that number, we replace the end (lower half of the image) of the Winwebsec family file with the ending of the Zbot family file that is that amount of bytes
5. This results in a Winwebsec family file obfuscated by the Zbot family file and the image is saved
6. Repeat steps from the beginning with the next Winwebsec family file until performed for all files in the Winwebsec family.

3.6   Gist Descriptors

"Gist descriptors" are features that were created in an effort to represent the "gist" of an image. Designed by A. Oliva and A. Torralba, that were trying to create what they called a "Spatial Envelope" [10]. This spatial envelope would represent the shape of a scene and nothing else; this means it should only contain what is essential to the image. Through experimentation, the authors were able to narrow down properties that would represent a spatial envelope as degrees of naturalness, openness, roughness, expansion, and ruggedness. These five properties would give a high-level representation of the scene and show the "gist" of it.

While gist descriptors have been used in many different applications, this research focuses on its use in malware classification. L. Nataraj et al. extract gist descriptors to use as their features in multiple experiments to classify malware [9]. They were able to obtain a classification accuracy of 98% when looking at a dataset that contained 25 malware families and a benign set of executables.

Our research is partially inspired by S. Yajamanam et al. [13]. In this previous work, the authors conducted a few experiments testing the robustness of gist descriptors. They obfuscated the malware, extracted the gist descriptors from the imaged versions of the obfuscated malware, and used a classification algorithm to classify them. However, the research by S. Yajamanam et al. was not focused on the robustness of gist descriptors, thus, there were only a few experiments to test robustness. To test the robustness of gist descriptors, they experimented with salting, an obfuscation technique that takes part of a different file and adds it to the malware in order to add noise and make it less identifiable. Three different experiments with salting were performed, that is, salting one family, salting with two closely related families, and salting all the malware families with benign samples. The experiments showed that the decline in accuracy due to the salting was not particularly evident. S. Yajamanam et al. concluded that, while there was the need of more experimentation, it seemed that gist descriptors was robust against this obfuscation technique.

In relation to the gist descriptor experiments, we first started with extracting the gist descriptors from the images. The gist descriptor features were then saved. They only need to be extracted once from each image [10].

To be able to compare our results with gist descriptors to the past works from [13] and [9], we used 320 gist descriptors instead of the full 512 gist descriptors that are extracted with the MATLAB code. These works had only used 320 gist descriptors because they wanted dimensions that have the global image properties with some of the local information.

4   Experiments and Results

These experiments are performed using the images that were created with the PIL. The first experiment classifies the images by applying CNN with all the family pairs.

The second and third experiments are the obfuscation experiments - with the second experiment testing the first salting method (random salting) while the third experiment tests the second salting method (contiguous salting). In these experiments, we performed binary classification. While the CNN uses the original images directly, the other four classification algorithms require to extract the gist descriptors first. With the gist descriptor experiments, a stratified 5-fold cross validation was used. These experiments were performed with a test split ratio of 0.2.

Here is the list of the tested ratios for the obfuscation set of experiments:

- 0%: accuracy obtained without any obfuscation
- 10%: accuracy obtained when 10% of the malware is salted by the other family
- 30%: accuracy obtained when 30% of the malware is salted by the other family
- 50%: accuracy obtained when 50% of the malware is salted by the other family
- 60%: accuracy obtained when 60% of the malware is salted by the other family
- 75%: accuracy obtained when 75% of the malware is salted by the other family
- 80%: accuracy obtained when 80% of the malware is salted by the other family
- 100%: accuracy obtained when 100% of the malware is salted by the other family.

In all of these experiments, we show the Winwebsec family. For binary classification experiments, we highlight the Winwebsec family versus the Zbot family.

4.1   Comparing Image Modes with CNN

The first set of experiments are a baseline to check what the classification accuracy is by using the CNN to classify the images that were simply created by the PIL. A binary classification was performed with the malware images created by the PIL. Different PIL image modes were used to experiment and understand how the modes would affect the accuracy.

An initial binary classification test with Winwebsec versus Zbot was performed with the different optimizers to check which gave the best result. We looked at few optimizer algorithms, that is, Root Mean Squared Propagation (RMSprop), Adaptive Moment Estimation (Adam), Stochastic Gradient Descent (SGD), Adadelta, and Adaptive Gradient (Adagrad). This initial test was performed with all the optimizers, a test split size of 0.2, and over five epochs. In Fig. 6, we see a comparison of the loss and accuracy values with the training and test data over the number of epochs. From Fig. 6 we determined that the Adam optimizer with three epochs is the best for this experiment. Thus, the rest of this experiment was performed with Adam optimizer, test split of 0.2, and over three epochs.

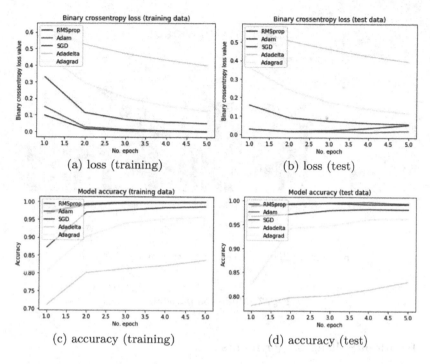

(a) loss (training)

(b) loss (test)

(c) accuracy (training)

(d) accuracy (test)

Fig. 6. Winwebsec vs Zbot (CNN and YCbCr modes)

Table 6 shows the binary classification results between Winwebsec and the other top five largest families of the dataset by using CNN. This set of experiments was also used to select the top two modes that we then applied for the rest of the experiments.

Table 6. Binary classification for Winwebsec

Mode	Zbot	Zeroaccess	Securityshield	Cridex
1	0.99687	0.99790	0.99665	0.99661
CMYK	0.99499	0.99790	0.99162	0.98134
L	0.99186	0.96003	0.97571	0.99406
RGB	0.98561	0.98247	0.99414	0.98134
YCbCr	0.99562	0.99439	0.99162	0.98388

Figure 7 shows a comparison between the modes and the accuracy ranking that they obtained. The ranking accuracy is the ranking that the accuracy value was in among the other modes. Rank 1 is the best while rank 5 is the worst. This means that the lower bars are better. From Fig. 7, we determine that mode 1 and mode YCbCr perform the best among the other modes.

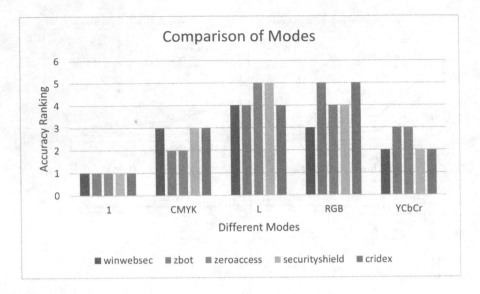

Fig. 7. Mode comparison

4.2 Random Salting Experiments

The second set of experiments introduces the first obfuscated technique. Specifically, we used the random salting method discussed in Sect. 3.5. Recall that for this salting technique, we randomly select bytes of another class to salt the executable before converting it to an image.

We experimented with CNN, k-NN, RF, SVM, and MLP classifiers and image modes 1, and YCbCr. In each case, we consider obfuscation rates of 0%, 10%, 30%, 50%, 60%, 75%, 80%, and 100%, and all experiments are based on an 80-20 training-test split.

For our CNN experiments, three training epochs are performed. We found that this obtains promising results without overfitting.

For k-NN, we needed to choose a value of k that avoids overfitting. Hence, we graphed accuracy versus the k value and looked for an "elbow" in the curve. After determining k, we used a grid search to find the best distance metric for each mode. We tested four distance metrics, namely, Euclidian, Manhattan, Chebyshev, and Minkowski.

For mode 1, we chose $k = 35$ based on Fig. 8(a). For mode YCbCr, we chose $k = 25$ based on Fig. 8(b). Based on a grid search, we found that the best distance metric for mode 1 and mode YCbCr is the Manhattan distance.

We now focus on using Random Forest to classify the malware based on the gist descriptors as features. To choose how many trees to use, we looked at the accuracy versus the number of estimators (number of trees). For mode 1, Fig. 9(a) suggests that 135 yields the best result, while for mode YCbCr, Fig. 9(b) shows that 160 is ideal.

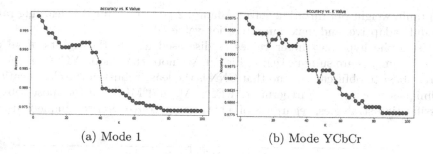

(a) Mode 1   (b) Mode YCbCr

Fig. 8. Accuracy of k-NN as a function of k

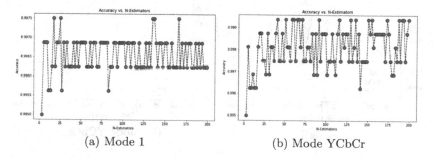

(a) Mode 1   (b) Mode YCbCr

Fig. 9. Random forest accuracy vs number of estimators

We then focused on using SVM to classify the malware based on the gist descriptors as features. We used a grid search to tune the hyperparameters. We tested regularization values of 0.1, 1, 10, 100, and 1000, and we tested gamma values of 1, 0.1, 0.01, 0.001, and 0.0001. We also tested linear, polynomial, radial basis function (RBF), and sigmoid kernel functions. For mode 1, we found that the best hyperparameters are regularization 10, gamma 0.001, and the RBF kernel. For YCbCr mode, we found regularization 10, gamma 0.01, and again the best kernel function is RBF.

Then, we implemented MLP to classify the malware samples based on the gist descriptors. We again used a grid search to tune the hyperparameters. We tested a few hidden layer activation functions, that is, identity, logistic, hyperbolic tangent (tanh), and rectified linear unit (ReLU). We tested the weight optimization solvers Quasi-Newton, Limited-memory BFGS (LBFGS), SGD, and Adam. We tested L2 penalty values of 0.1, 0.01, 0.05, 0.001, and 0.0001, and we tested learning rate schedules constant, invscaling, and adaptive. We also tested maximum iterations of 50, 100, 150, and 200.

With mode 1, we found that the best hyperparameters are hidden layer activation function ReLU, weight optimization solver LBFGS, L2 penalty value 0.001, learning rate schedule invscaling, and maximum iteration value 200. With mode YCbCr, the best hyperparameters are hidden layer activation function tanh, weight optimization solver Adam, L2 penalty value 0.1, learning rate schedule adaptive, and maximum iteration value 50.

Using the hyperparameter values as discussed above, the results of all of our experiments are summarized in Fig. 10. We note that mode YCbCr is much more robust to obfuscation, and that CNN is the least robust of the classification techniques considered. Furthermore, RF, SVM, and MLP are the most robust classification strategies, regardless of which image conversion technique is used.

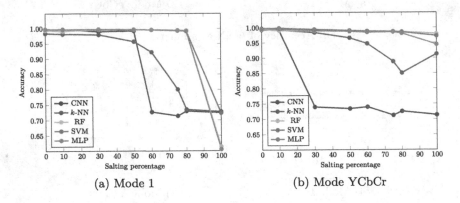

(a) Mode 1   (b) Mode YCbCr

Fig. 10. Winwebsec vs Zbot (gist descriptors, random salting)

4.3   Contiguous Salting

The third set of experiments uses the contiguous salting method, that is, we salt executables with contiguous bytes from another class. These experiments use the same classifiers and the same hyperparameters tuning approach as discussed in the previous Section. We omit the hyperparameter tuning details and describe directly the results of our experiments.

Our contiguous salting experiments are summarized in Fig. 11. We see that mode YCbCr is extremely robust with respect to this method of salting. As with random salting, we observed that CNN is the least robust of the classification techniques.

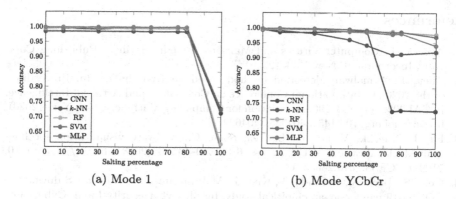

(a) Mode 1   (b) Mode YCbCr

Fig. 11. Winwebsec vs Zbot (gist descriptors, contiguous salting)

4.4 CNN Experiments Without Obfuscation

The first experiment with CNN showed that CNN yields good results in binary classification. In all the binary classification combinations with the top five largest families in the Malicia dataset, nearly all of the accuracies are more than 92%. There are only three pairs from the first experiment that yielded low results.

This set of experiments was performed to decide the best modes to use for the rest of the experiments. While we chose mode 1 and mode YCbCr to use since they yielded the best accuracies, the other modes were often close in accuracy.

5   Conclusion and Future Work

From the results of the experiments performed in this research, we found that using gist descriptors extracted from the images is a more robust approach than directly applying a CNN to images. In fact, the experiments showed that the CNN did not obtain the same high accuracies as the classifiers that instead relied on the gist descriptors.

When experimenting with the different modes, we found that mode YCbCr and mode 1 yielded the best results in combination with the gist descriptors. In particular, with mode YCbCr, we were able to obtain the best accuracy for higher obfuscation percentages, as compared to mode 1.

Future work could focus on testing different obfuscation methods. Regarding the salting technique itself, more experiments could be performed testing different methods of salting. This research focused on bytes, while a different method may obtain different accuracy results with other image modes. Finally, other image modes could also be considered.

References

1. Aycock, J.: Computer Viruses and Malware, 1st edn. Springer Publishing Company, Incorporated, New York (2010)
2. Chen, J.: A malware detection method based on RGB image. In: Proceedings of the 2020 6th International Conference on Computing and Artificial Intelligence, ICCAI 2020, pp. 283–290. Association for Computing Machinery, New York (2020). https://doi.org/10.1145/3404555.3404622
3. Fu, J., Xue, J., Wang, Y., Liu, Z., Shan, C.: Malware visualization for fine-grained classification. IEEE Access 6, 14510–14523 (2018). https://doi.org/10.1109/ACCESS.2018.2805301
4. Gero, S., Back, S., LaPrade, J., Kim, J.: Malware infections in the US during the COVID-19 pandemic: an empirical study. Int. J. Cybersecurity Intell. Cybercrime 4, 25–37 (2021)
5. Han, K., Kang, B., Im, E.G.: Malware analysis using visualized image matrices. Sci. World J. 2014, 132713 (2014). https://doi.org/10.1155/2014/132713
6. Lundh, F., Clark, A.: Concepts (2022). https://pillow.readthedocs.io/en/stable/handbook/concepts.html
7. Mbaabu, O.: Introduction to random forest in machine learning (2020). https://www.section.io/engineering-education/introduction-to-random-forest-in-machine-learning/
8. Nappa, A., Rafique, M.Z., Caballero, J.: The MALICIA dataset: identification and analysis of drive-by download operations. Int. J. Inf. Secur. 14(1), 15–33 (2014). https://doi.org/10.1007/s10207-014-0248-7
9. Nataraj, L., Karthikeyan, S., Jacob, G., Manjunath, B.S.: Malware images: visualization and automatic classification. In: Proceedings of the 8th International Symposium on Visualization for Cyber Security, VizSec 2011. Association for Computing Machinery, New York (2011). https://doi.org/10.1145/2016904.2016908
10. Oliva, A., Torralba, A.: Modeling the shape of the scene: a holistic representation of the spatial envelope. Int. J. Comput. Vision 42, 145–175 (2004). http://people.csail.mit.edu/torralba/code/spatialenvelope/
11. Stamp, M.: Introduction to Machine Learning with Applications in Information Security, 2nd edn. Chapman & Hall/CRC, Boca Raton (2022)
12. Vasan, D., Alazab, M., Wassan, S., Naeem, H., Safaei, B., Zheng, Q.: IMCFN: image-based malware classification using fine-tuned convolutional neural network architecture. Comput. Netw. 171, 107138 (2020). https://doi.org/10.1016/j.comnet.2020.107138. https://www.sciencedirect.com/science/article/pii/S1389128619304736
13. Yajamanam, S., Selvin, V.R.S., Troia, F.D., Stamp, M.: Deep learning versus gist descriptors for image-based malware classification. In: Mori, P., Furnell, S., Camp, O. (eds.) Proceedings of the 4th International Conference on Information Systems Security and Privacy, ICISSP 2018, pp. 553–561. SciTePress (2018)
14. Yakura, H., Shinozaki, S., Nishimura, R., Oyama, Y., Sakuma, J.: Malware analysis of imaged binary samples by convolutional neural network with attention mechanism. In: Proceedings of the Eighth ACM Conference on Data and Application Security and Privacy, CODASPY 2018, pp. 127–134. Association for Computing Machinery, New York (2018). https://doi.org/10.1145/3176258.3176335

Word Embeddings for Fake Malware Generation

Quang Duy Tran and Fabio Di Troia[✉]

San José State University, San Jose, USA
fabio.ditroia@sjsu.edu

Abstract. Signature and anomaly-based techniques are the fundamental methods to detect malware. However, in recent years this type of threat has advanced to become more complex and sophisticated, making these techniques less effective. For this reason, researchers have resorted to state-of-the-art machine learning techniques to combat the threat of information security. Nevertheless, despite the integration of the machine learning models, there is still a shortage of data in training that prevents these models from performing at their peak. In the past, generative models have been found to be highly effective at generating image-like data that are similar to the actual data distribution. In this paper, we leverage the knowledge of generative modeling on opcode sequences and aim to generate malware samples by taking advantage of the contextualized embeddings from BERT. We obtained promising results when differentiating between real and generated samples. We observe that generated malware has such similar characteristics to actual malware that the classifiers are having difficulty in distinguishing between the two, in which the classifiers falsely identify the generated malware as actual malware almost 90% of the time.

Keywords: BERT · GAN · Malware · Malware detection · Word embedding

1 Introduction

The term malware refers to software that is created with the intention of causing damage to computer data [2]. According to Statista, a total of 5.6 billion malware attacks took place worldwide in 2020 [15]. These attacks target many small and large industries, such as finance, transportation, healthcare, manufacturing, or professional, which can cause immeasurable damage. For this reason, malware prevention has become a vital part of information security.

Recently, machine learning approaches have been utilized in the malware detection area to combat these threats. The common method of training intelligent models is by collecting the malware characteristics such as opcode sequences, API calls, and bytes vectors, among others [3]. Despite the promising results from machine learning techniques, there are still significant obstacles

© The Author(s) 2022
L. Bathen et al. (Eds.): SVCC 2022, CCIS 1683, pp. 22–37, 2022.
https://doi.org/10.1007/978-3-031-24049-2_2

to overcome, such as adversarial machine learning to deceive machine learning models [17], malware code obfuscation [5], and the shortage of publicly available training datasets [28].

In this research, we build realistic fake malware samples from seven distinct malware families by applying Wasserstein Generative Adversarial Network with Gradient Penalty (WGAN-GP). To build such realistic samples of a malware infection, it is crucial to identify the distinctive features of each malware family [33]. In general, malware samples belonging to the same family share many characteristics with one another, yet they differ from those belonging to other families. These unique characteristics of a malware sample can be quantified by word embeddings, which can be generated by many Natural Language Processing (NLP) models, including BERT. Thus, the focus of this study is on the effectiveness of word embeddings developed in the context of creating malware samples. We employ a variety of machine learning classification techniques, including One-Class Support Vector Machine (OCSVM), Isolation Forest, and Local Outlier Factor, to assess this effectiveness by differentiating between real and generated samples.

The rest of the paper is structured as follows. Section 2 reviews earlier and related work. In addition, it provides a brief overview of the machine learning techniques and concepts employed in this study. Section 3 explains our methodology, including our malware creation pipeline, and the training and evaluation procedure. Section 4 discusses the actual implementation and our experimental setup. Section 5 contains the analysis and results of our experiments. Finally, in Sect. 6, we present the conclusions and future directions of this paper.

2   Background

In this section, we discuss related work in applying Generative Adversarial Networks (GANs) to generate malware samples. Also, we briefly introduce the machine learning techniques used in this research.

2.1   Selective Survey of Related Work

Creating images from malware executable files and utilizing them to perform malware detection and classification is a current trend in modern malware research. This enables the use of image-analysis techniques, as well as the operations of strong deep neural networks that function well with images. Many researchers utilized malware images to produce malware samples for generative models, since it allows them to add more samples to the pool and even to perform data augmentation on real data. For instance, in [21] the authors applied Variational Auto Encoder (VAE) and GANs to expand the training dataset using malware as images, resulting in 2% and 6% increase in accuracy, respectively. Another similar study [29] implemented GAN for the same purpose and obtained a 6% increase in accuracy when trained ResNet-18 model on malware data.

Although treating malware as images and perform augmentation has gained popularity, we should not ignore the drawback of this technique, which requires huge computational resources. Additionally, training and testing deep convolutional networks can be computational expensive and time-consuming. Understanding the disadvantages, the authors in [31] proposed another approach based on generating mnemonic opcode sequences by applying and comparing Hidden Markov Models and three different GAN architectures. They were able to fool the classifiers in distinguishing between real and generated malware with a 76% detection/accuracy score when using WGAN-GP. Their main goal, however, was to experiment with various generative modeling techniques when building mnemonic opcode sequences to represent fake malware. In this work, we push further the previous study by introducing word embedding generation. The main difference between our study and [31] is that we utilize word embedding technique to generate realistic malware. Even though our approach is very similar to [31], we will not compare our results to theirs because our evaluation method is different.

Natural Language Processing (NLP) techniques can extract rich information from sentences in a language, known as word embeddings. These embeddings are able, for instance, to capture the meaning of a phrase, construct sentences with similar meaning, or fill in the blanks within a sentence. NLP models extract information about a word's relationship to every other word in a phrase. The model then clusters words with similar meanings together in a higher dimensional space. This information assists NLP models in performing classification and prediction tasks. In the realm of malicious malware, the models are utilized to build embeddings for malware samples. For example, a research [25] was conducted on detecting malware samples by applying NLP to mnemonic opcode sequences. The results, derived by utilizing word embeddings generated by Word2Vec, HMM2Vec, ELMo, and BERT, prove that NLP based models can extract rich features that assist with classification accuracy. In particular, word embeddings generated by BERT consistently achieved a superior classification accuracy compared to other NLP techniques, with an accuracy of around 96%.

We see that there is a gap in the literature when it comes to utilizing word embeddings to assist GAN to generate realistic malware. As a result, we conduct a study on this subject by introducing the usage of BERT in generative modeling. In summary, we extract mnemonic opcodes from malware files, apply BERT transformer to obtain embeddings, and train generative models to generate malware embeddings.

2.2 Machine Learning Techniques

In this section, we discuss the key elements of this paper, that is, the generative and NLP models. The generative model that we implemented is Wasserstein GAN with Gradient Penalty (WGAN-GP), while the NLP model is BERT.

Wasserstein GAN with Gradient Penalty. Ishaan Gulrajani et al. introduced WGAN-GP in 2017 [32]. The fundamental goal of this design is to surpass

WGAN's disadvantage by applying gradient norm penalty with Wasserstein loss formulation to achieve Lipschitz continuity. The authors provide Corollary 1, which states that the optimum critic in WGAN has a gradient norm of 1 and is 1-Lipschitz continuous. Taking advantage of this, a "penalty" is placed on the critic if the norm of its gradient deviates from the value 1. WGAN-GP training method is similar to the WGAN algorithm, with the exception of the weight clipping and the inclusion of the gradient penalty [32]. More details about WGAN can be found in [26].

BERT. Bidirectional Encoder Representations from Transformers (BERT) is a transformer-based NLP model that has shown to be successful in difficult language-based tasks such as masked word prediction and sentiment classification. The model is capable of creating contextualized word embedding by taking the context in which the individual words are used into account. BERT model finds word relationships via attention, a method that aids in the retention of long-term dependencies in sentences of up to 512 words, as shown in Fig. 1. In general, a normal language phrase does not exceed 512 words, but the opcode sequences in a malware sample can surpass this limit. In our testing, the first 400 opcodes from each malware file were adequate to obtain satisfactory outcomes while using less computational resources. Further details on the architecture and attention mechanism of BERT can be found in [16], while an analysis of its attention heads is covered in [7].

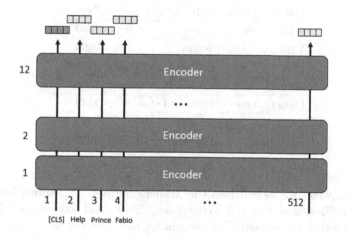

Fig. 1. Trained BERT components

DistilBERT. Despite the fact that BERT has grown more common in Natural Language Processing, running these huge pre-trained models with tight computational training or inference budgets remains difficult. DistilBERT, a computationally efficient and lightweight version of BERT, was proposed to overcome this challenge. DistilBERT model was constructed using the knowledge distillation during the pre-training phase to shrink a BERT model by 40%, while preserving 97% of its language comprehension skills and being 60% faster [4]. This model, similar to its larger counterparts, is also capable of being fine-tuned with good performances on a wide range of tasks. Seeing the advantages the model offers, we utilized DistilBERT in our study to create contextualized malware embeddings. The DistilBERT model that we used is hosted and open sourced by HuggingFace team [6], and was pre-trained on the English language. In this study, the model was neither trained nor fine-tuned on malware samples. More details about the model can be found in [4].

3   Methodology

This section provide details on the dataset, as well as the training and evaluation procedure we followed in our experiments.

3.1   Dataset

The dataset that we used for all of our experiments consists of seven malware families with more than 1000 samples (shown in Table 1).

Table 1. Dataset summary

Malware family	Type	Samples
WinWebSec	Rogue	4360
VBInject	Worm	2694
Zbot	Information Stealer	2136
Renos	Trojan Downloader	1568
OnLineGames	Password stealer	1513
BHO	Trojan	1405
Zeroaccess	Corrupting Devices	1305

To begin with, we looked into the Malicia dataset [18], which has over 50 malware families, and selected Winwebsec, Zbot, and Zeroaccess since they have over 1000 samples each. The remaining four families were obtained from VirusShare [30]. There are over 120,000 malware executables in this 100 Gigabytes dataset, from which four extra families were selected, namely, VBInject, Renos, OnLineGames, and BHO. These families are in top 5 most sample counts, where each has more than 1300 samples. Winwebsec and Zbot are also provided in the VirusShare dataset. However, we use the ones from Malicia dataset because they have almost double the sample size.

We utilized *objdump*, *sed*, and *cut*, the command-line utilities included in the GNU Binary Utilities package for Unix-like operating systems. Using *objdump*, executable files can be disassembled into Assembly code, thus allowing them to be extracted as mnemonic opcodes. Then, *sed* and *cut* can be used to filter and transform text to remove all the excessive information, such as registers or addresses.

Here is a short description of our selected malware families.

Winwebsec: a trojan that creates fictitious problems and claims to have solutions that are authentic anti-virus software [8].

Zbot: a trojan that breaches into Microsoft Window computers and steals confidential information [9].

Zeroaccess: a trojan that infects Window computers and exploits them for malicious purposes such as corrupting devices [10].

BHO: performs a wide range of harmful behaviors as directed by an attacker [14]

OnLineGames: steals users' login credentials and records keystroke activity [12]

Renos: pretends that the machine is infected with malware and demands money to remove the non-existed spyware [13]

VBInject: packed malware that obfuscates its content to conceal other malware and itself from detection [11]

3.2   Training Procedure

Figure 2 depicts an example of our WGAN-GP training process. Tokenizers are applied to the original malware dataset before turning into BERT inputs that generate word embeddings. These embeddings are then directly used to train the generative model. After training, WGAN-GP is able to generate fake malware embeddings as outputs. We rinse and repeat this entire process through all malware families.

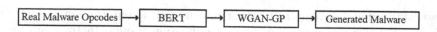

Fig. 2. WGAN-GP training process

3.3   Evaluation Procedure

Figure 3 shows an illustration of our WGAN-GP evaluation procedure. The initial set up is partially the same as the training procedure, where we generated real malware embeddings from malware opcodes using DistilBERT model. Following, we apply 5-fold cross-validation and split the data into 80% training and 20% validation set. Test data contains malware embeddings generated by WGAN-GP, and is split into five subsets to participate in 5-fold cross-validation. After, we construct three new classifiers (One-Class SVM, Isolation Forest, and Local Outlier Factor) inside each fold to train and assess on the validation and test dataset. At the end of each fold, we obtain train, validation, and test accuracy. Next, we calculate the average of the 5 folds as the final results for that WGAN-GP model. We cycle over all generative models that were trained on that same malware family, and compare their results to determine which model has the lowest test accuracy score. The lowest score indicates that the model was the most successful in generating fake samples able to confuse the detection algorithms. Such model is, thus, selected as the best generative model for that particular malware family. This same process is repeated for all malware families.

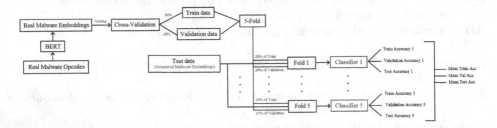

Fig. 3. WGAN-GP evaluation process

4   Implementation

In this section, we discuss the techniques we applied to extract embeddings using BERT model. Moreover, the parameters used for the generative and classification models are also provided.

4.1   Feature Extraction

The classification tokens (CLS) gather information about the entire sentence and are used to express sentence-level classification results. In the instance of a malware sample, the CLS token collects all of the sample's information. This information can be used to aid the learning of WGAN-GP. Therefore, among the 768 hidden units of BERT, the first column (that represents the CLS tokens) is selected. Furthermore, leveraging image scaling from image processing, we applied the same principle to BERT embeddings to help ease the learning of WGAN-GP. The embeddings were also scaled to fit into the range of -1 and $+1$. This technique simplifies BERT embeddings, which allows the generative models to convert faster.

4.2 WGAN with Gradient Penalty

In our study, we took WGAN-GP into consideration because the network has been shown to perform well in [31]. We were influenced by the study of the authors in [31], and used the same parameters in our experiments. Adam optimizer was used with the following parameters:

$$Adam(lr = 0.0001, \beta_1 = 0.5, \beta_2 = 0.9)$$

Each WGAN-GP model was trained for 100,000 epochs. The critic network consists of three hidden Conv1D layers with 64, 128, and 256 filters and a kernel size of 3. Similarly, a kernel size of 3 and three Conv1D layers with 64, 32, and 16 filters were utilized in the generator network. LeakyReLU is the activation functions for the hidden layers of Conv1D.

In the generator, the output layer consists of a fully connected Dense layer with 768 neurons. The reason to use exactly 768 neurons is to match the output size of BERT. The activation function for the generator is TanH, while there is none for the critic network. The authors in [31] decided to not implement neither Batch Normalization nor Layer Normalization in the critic network. But in the generator, Batch Normalization is still applied.

The penalty coefficient, λ, is set to 10. The parameter "n_critic", which represents the number of critic iterations per generator iteration, is set to 100. In other words, for each epoch, the generator was only updated after training the critic for 100 iterations. Table 2 shows all the parameters and their values used in the generator and critic.

Table 2. Generator and Critic parameters

	Parameter	Value
Generator	activation	TanH
	kernel_size	3
	Conv1D_layer_filter_1	64
	Conv1D_layer_filter_2	32
	Conv1D_layer_filter_3	16
	Conv1D_padding	same
	BatchNorm_momentum	0.8
Critic	activation	LeakyReLU
	kernel_size	3
	Conv1D_layer_filter_1	64
	Conv1D_layer_filter_2	128
	Conv1D_layer_filter_3	256
	Conv1D_padding	same

4.3 Evaluation Implementation

Because GAN are most commonly used in the image domain, the two popular metrics Inception Score [22] and Fréchet Inception Distance (FID) [27] are
used to evaluate the quality of the generated images. In addition, generated
images are saved every few hundred epochs, such as 500, before being examined
visually. However, our dataset consists of opcode sequences, which are impossi-
ble to be inspected visually. Hence, we applied a different metrics to evaluate
GAN performance. Reading about the two scores, we realized that the similarity
between them is that they are calculated using the inception-v3 model. Moreover, inception-v3 was trained on more than a million images from the ImageNet
database, and attained a greater than 78.1% accuracy on the same dataset [1].
The key point here is that, when evaluating against GAN, the inception-v3 network has neither seen nor learned about the generated images. Therefore, we
decided to not include generated data, but only malware data, into our training
set. We then use three classification models, that is, One-Class SVM (OCSVM)
[23], Isolation Forest [20], and Local Outlier Factor (LoF) [24], which are based
on the idea of anomaly detection, to evaluate GAN's performance.

Anomaly detection can be branched off into outlier and novelty detection.
To decide which one to use, we have to look into the difference between the
two. Outlier detection is used when there are outliers in the training data, which
are observations that are different from the rest of the data [19]. On the other
hands, novelty detection is used when the training data is not contaminated with
outliers, and we are interested in determining if a new observation is an outlier
[19]. Since our train data only contains malware opcodes, novelty detection is
selected in our evaluation. Our test dataset, which only contains generated data,
will be considered as new observations to be determined if it is anomaly.

In our study, we saved the generative model at every 500 epochs. We then
generated fake samples from all saved generative models, and classified if they
are outliers or not using the three classification models. Afterwards, we tuned
all three classifiers using sklearn GridSearchCV [34] on each malware family to
achieve the highest train and validation accuracy. Upon training on the real malware data using 5-fold cross validation, these classifiers will be evaluated against
the generated data. Accuracy score is then computed to see how similar the generated data is when compared to the real malware data. Lastly, we compared the
score across all our generative models and pick out the best model. Note that our
goal is to achieve as low accuracy score as possible. High accuracy shows that
the three classifiers classified generated data as outliers, which is not similar to
real malware data. And vice versa, low accuracy means the classifiers classified
generated samples as inliers, which is similar to real malware data. Table 3, 4
and 5 below are the summary of the tuned parameters we used for the classifiers.

Table 3. One-class SVM parameters

Malware family	Parameters		
	nu	kernel	gamma
Winwebsec	0.5	sigmoid	0.1
Zbot	0.01	sigmoid	0.001
Zeroaccess	0.01	sigmoid	0.001
VBInject	0.01	poly	0.3
BHO	0.01	rbf	0.3
Renos	0.01	rbf	0.01
OnLineGames	0.01	poly	0.3

Table 4. Isolation forest parameters

Malware family	Parameters			
	contamination	max_samples	n_estimators	bootstrap
Winwebsec	0.01	auto	1	False
Zbot	0.01	auto	1	True
Zeroaccess	0.01	auto	1	True
VBInject	0.01	auto	1	True
BHO	0.01	0.5	1	True
Renos	0.01	auto	0.8	True
OnLineGames	0.01	auto	1	True

Table 5. Local outlier factor parameters

Malware family	Parameters					
	p	contamination	leaf_size	n_neighbors	algorithm	novelty
Winwebsec	2	0.01	2	50	auto	True
Zbot	1	0.01	2	30	auto	True
Zeroaccess	1	0.01	2	30	auto	True
VBInject	1	0.01	2	5	auto	True
BHO	1	0.01	2	30	auto	True
Renos	1	0.01	2	5	auto	True
OnLineGames	2	0.01	2	5	auto	True

5   Results

This section provides the classification results of our experiments followed by a detailed analysis.

5.1   Evaluation Score

The author in [32] suggested that the critic's loss, which is used to assess WGAN-GP's performance, should start at a high negative value and then converge to zero. The generator's loss, on the other hand, can fluctuate and, hence, is not intuitive. Therefore, we start by looking at the loss curves and then the classification results.

The critic loss curves for seven families presented a similar pattern to the one in [31]. In our experiments, they all started at around -10, then quickly spiked up to around -27 during the first 50 epochs, and slowly converted to around -0.19 after $10,000$ epochs. In other words, our model was trained properly when it exhibited this behavior. Figure 4 below shows the ranking (from worst to best) of critic loss on all malware families at the end of training.

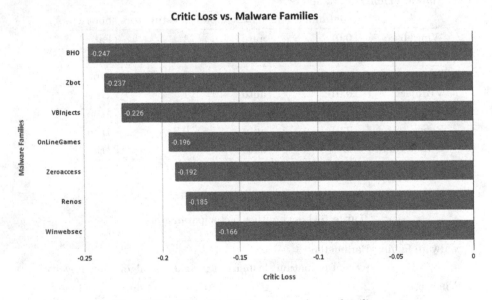

Fig. 4. Ranking of critic loss on malware families

The best test accuracy scores were selected independently from all generative models, the seven malware families, and the three types of classifiers. Our parameters for each classifier were the same as those discussed in Table 3, 4, and 5. The average training accuracy score across seven families was roughly 99.1%. The average validation accuracy score was roughly the same as training accuracy, about 99%. However, the test accuracy score is consistently low, achieved the highest score of 38.8% with BHO, and the lowest score of 0.00%

with Renos. The average of the test score across all families was 15.6%. One-Class SVM showed to perform better than Isolation Forest and Local Outlier Factor in terms of classifying between the real and generated malware data. Most of the test accuracy scores obtained by OCSVM were over 0.00%, except for Renos family.

The Isolation Forest Classifier obtained an average training accuracy of 99.4%. The average validation accuracy score was around 99.4%, which was similar to the training accuracy. However, unlike OCSVM, Isolation Forest obtained lower average test accuracy score (about 2.5%). There are a few more families having the test accuracy scores closer to zero compared to OCSVM.

The average of training and validation accuracy scores of Local Outlier Factor are 99.4% and 98.9%, respectively. There are more families that fooled the classifier that could not distinguish between real and generated malware data. BHO, however, obtained the highest test accuracy in all three classifiers (38.8% for OCSVM, 14.4% for Isolation Forest, and 75.7% for Local Outlier Factor). The complexity and lack of samples for the BHO family could be a big contributing factor to this result. Having the second least amount of samples, 1405 data points, WGAN-GP was not able to adequately learn the distribution of this family. This is further supported by having the highest negative critic loss (-0.247) in the training procedure compared to other families. We computed the average accuracy from all test score, and obtained a 12.12% average accuracy. Table 6 summarized the comparison of the accuracy score between each family and classifier. We see that the majority of the families were recreated correctly by our BERT-GAN approach, with the exception of the BHO family for which a considerable number of samples were still classified as fake by LoF and OCSVM.

5.2 Further Analysis

To understand the importance of the accuracy score, we should take a look at its formula:

$$Accuracy = \frac{TruePositive + TrueNegative}{TruePositive + FalsePositive + TrueNegative + FalseNegative}$$

In our case, *Positive* represents real malware and *Negative* represents generated malware. Since our test dataset only contains generated malware, *True Positive* is always 0, that is, cases that are correctly classified as real malware. Similarly, *False Negative* is always 0. Hence, the formula simplified as follow:

$$Accuracy = \frac{TrueNegative}{TrueNegative + FalsePositive}$$

The new formula measures the true negative rate, which is the classifiers' ability to predict a true negative of each category available. Thus, when we achieved 12.12% average accuracy, this tells us that the classifiers are only able to correctly identify generated malware 12% of the time. In other words, if we run the evaluation to classify between real and generated malware 100 times,

Table 6. WGAN with gradient penalty scores.

Malware Family	One Class SVM			Isolation Forest			Local Outlier Factor		
	Train	Val	Test	Train	Val	Test	Train	Val	Test
Winwebsec	0.995	0.995	0.044	0.998	0.998	0.0	0.993	0.992	0.0
Zbot	0.991	0.990	0.125	0.992	0.996	0.006	0.992	0.991	0.081
Zeroaccess	0.989	0.989	0.163	0.998	0.996	0.0	0.992	0.989	0.0
BHO	0.983	0.981	0.388	0.992	0.992	0.144	0.994	0.994	0.756
OnLineGames	0.994	0.994	0.219	0.992	0.99	0.006	0.996	0.989	0.438
VBInject	0.993	0.992	0.156	0.995	0.995	0.006	0.995	0.989	0.0
Renos	0.99	0.99	0.0	0.994	0.994	0.013	0.998	0.983	0.0

the classifiers will falsely classify generated malware as actual malware 88 times. Low true negative rate shows that generated malware has such similar characteristics to actual malware that the classifiers are having difficulty in distinguishing between the two. Moreover, the results of the experiments look promising since we applied k-fold cross validation to reduce the effects of overfitting.

6   Conclusions and Future Work

In this paper, we aimed at taking advantage of contextualized embeddings created by BERT to generate fake malware embeddings. The generative model we utilized was Wasserstein Generative Adversarial Networks with Gradient Penalty (WGAN-GP).

In previous studies, GANs have been shown to generate fake malware opcode sequences. In term of generating malware embeddings, however, there exists a gap in the literature.

We explored that gap in our study by training the generative models on malware embeddings and assess them with three classification models, namely, One-Class SVM (OCSVM), Isolation Forest, and Local Outlier Factor (LoF). The results obtained in our experiments show that WGAN-GP can generate malware embeddings that can closely match the real data distribution. This demonstrates that WGAN-GP algorithms can be successfully applied to produce malware embeddings in addition to generating image data. In some cases, generative models could help increasing the number of data samples for families with limited sample size. This new approach improves the quality of the fake malware generated by GAN algorithms, and creates more encouraging opportunities to apply such data to enhance malware datasets used to train supervised machine learning models.

For future work, this paper may be taken in a variety of different directions. The dataset, for example, may be expanded, and the experiments can include a greater number of malware families. A multi-class generative model can also be explored instead of training distinct WGAN-GP models for each family. Another possible application is to use many different word embeddings techniques to support WGAN-GP training, such as Word2Vec, ELMo, or different version of BERT. Training BERT model on malware dataset before generating embeddings could also be considered, which may possibly boost the learning of generative models. Finally, because stateful networks can produce intriguing results, experiments using LSTM-GAN can be performed.

References

1. Advanced guide to inception V3, Google. https://cloud.google.com/tpu/docs/inception-v3-advanced
2. Aycock, J.: Computer Viruses and Malware. Springer, New York (2006)
3. Dhanasekar, D., Di Troia, F., Potika, K., Stamp, M.: Detecting encrypted and polymorphic malware using hidden Markov models. In: Parkinson, S., Crampton, A., Hill, R. (eds.) Guide to Vulnerability Analysis for Computer Networks and Systems. CCN, pp. 281–299. Springer, Cham (2018). https://doi.org/10.1007/978-3 319-92624-7_12
4. Sanh, V., Debut, L., Chaumond, J., Wolf, T.: DistilBERT, a distilled version of BERT: smaller, faster, cheaper and lighter. ArXiv, abs/1910.01108 (2019)
5. O'Kane, P., Sezer, S., McLaughlin, K.: Obfuscation: the hidden malware. IEEE Secur. Priv. **9**(5), 41–47 (2011). https://doi.org/10.1109/MSP.2011.98
6. Hugging Face. Distilbert. https://huggingface.co/transformers/model_doc/distilbert.html
7. Clark, K., Khandelwal, U., Levy, O., Manning, C.: What does BERT look at? an analysis of BERT's attention. In: Proceedings of the 2019 ACL Workshop BlackboxNLP: Analyzing and Interpreting Neural Networks for NLP, Florence, Italy, August 2019, pp. 276–286. Association for Computational Linguistics (2019)
8. Microsoft Security Intelligence. Winwebsec (2010). https://www.microsoft.com/security/portal/threat/encyclopedia/entry.aspx?Name=Win32%2fWinwebsec
9. Microsoft Security Intelligence. Zbot (2010). https://www.microsoft.com/en-us/wdsi/threats/malware-encyclopedia-description?name=win32%2Fzbot
10. Asher-Dotan, L.: What is zero access malware, cybereason i cybersecurity software to end cyber attacks, 16-May-2016. https://www.cybereason.com/blog/what-is-zeroaccess-malware
11. Microsoft Security Intelligence. VBInject (2010). https://www.microsoft.com/en-us/wdsi/threats/malware-encyclopedia-description?Name=VirTool:Win32/VBInject%26ThreatID=-2147367171
12. Microsoft Security Intelligence. Onlinegames (2008). https://www.microsoft.com/en-us/wdsi/threats/malware-encyclopedia-description?Name=PWS%3AWin32%2FOnLineGames
13. Microsoft Security Intelligence. Renos (2006). https://www.microsoft.com/en-us/wdsi/threats/malware-encyclopedia-description?Name=TrojanDownloader:Win32/Renos&threatId=16054
14. Microsoft Security Intelligence. BHO (2020). https://www.microsoft.com/en-us/wdsi/threats/malware-encyclopedia-description?Name=Trojan:Win32/BHO.BO
15. Johnson, J.: Number of malware attacks per year 2020, Statista, 20-Aug-2021. https://www.statista.com/statistics/873097/malware-attacks-per-year-worldwide/
16. Vaswani, A., et al.: Attention is all you need (2017). https://arxiv.org/abs/1706.03762

17. Huang, L., Joseph, A.D., Nelson, B., Rubinstein, B.I., Tygar, J.D.: Adversarial machine learning. In: Proceedings of the 4th ACM Workshop on Security and Artificial Intelligence, pp. 43–58 (2011)
18. Nappa, A., Rafique, M.Z., Caballero, J.: The MALICIA dataset: identification and analysis of drive-by download operations. Int. J. Inf. Secur. **14**(1), 15–33 (2015). https://doi.org/10.1007/s10207-014-0248-7
19. "novelty and outlier detection", scikit-learn. https://scikit-learn.org/stable/modules/outlier_detection.html
20. Liu, F.T., Ting, K.M., Zhou, Z.: Isolation forest. Eighth IEEE Int. Conf. Data Min. **2008**, 413–422 (2008). https://doi.org/10.1109/ICDM.2008.17
21. Burks, R., Islam, K.A., Lu, Y., Li, J.: Data augmentation with generative models for improved malware detection: a comparative study. In: 2019 IEEE 10th Annual Ubiquitous Computing, Electronics Mobile Communication Conference (UEMCON), pp. 0660–0665 (2019). https://doi.org/10.1109/UEMCON47517.2019.8993085
22. Salimans, T., Goodfellow, I., Zaremba, W., Cheung, V., Radford, A., Chen, X.: Improved techniques for training GANs (2016)
23. Bounsiar, A., Madden, M.G.: One-class support vector machines revisited. In: International Conference on Information Science & Applications (ICISA) 2014, pp. 1–4 (2014). https://doi.org/10.1109/ICISA.2014.6847442
24. Pokrajac, D., Lazarevic, A., Latecki, L.J.: Incremental local outlier detection for data streams. In: IEEE Symposium on Computational Intelligence and Data Mining 2007, pp. 504–515 (2007). https://doi.org/10.1109/CIDM.2007.368917
25. Kale, A.S., Pandya, V., Di Troia, F., et al.: Malware classification with Word2Vec, HMM2Vec, BERT, and ELMo. J. Comput. Virol. Hack. Tech. (2022). https://doi.org/10.1007/s11416-022-00424-3
26. Arjovsky, M., Chintala, S., Bottou, L.: Wasserstein GAN (2017)
27. Heusel, M., Ramsauer, H., Unterthiner, T., Nessler, B., Hochreiter, S.: GANs trained by a two time-scale update rule converge to a local Nash equilibrium. In: Proceedings of the 31st International Conference on Neural Information Processing Systems, NIPS 2017, pp. 6629–6640. Curran Associates Inc. (2017)
28. Gibert, D., Mateu, C., Planes, J.: The rise of machine learning for detection and classification of malware: research developments, trends and challenges. J. Netw. Comput. Appl. **153**, 102526 (2020). https://doi.org/10.1016/j.jnca.2019.102526, https://www.sciencedirect.com/science/article/pii/S1084804519303868
29. Lu, Y., Li, J.: Generative adversarial network for improving deep learning based malware classification. In: 2019 Winter Simulation Conference (WSC), pp. 584–593 (2019). https://doi.org/10.1109/WSC40007.2019.9004932
30. Roberts, J.M.: VirusShare.com - Because Sharing is Caring (2011). http://www.virusshare.com
31. Harshit, T.: Fake malware opcodes generation using HMM and different GAN algorithms (2021). Master's Projects. 1001. https://doi.org/10.31979/etd.eq6a-twvq, https://scholarworks.sjsu.edu/etd_projects/1001
32. Gulrajani, I., Ahmed, F., Arjovsky, M., Dumoulin, V., Courville, A.: Improved training of wasserstein GANs (2017)
33. Basole, S., Di Troia, F., Stamp, M.: Multifamily malware models. J. Comput. Virol. Hacking Tech. **16**(1), 79–92 (2020). https://doi.org/10.1007/s11416-019-00345-8
34. sklearn. Gridsearchcv. https://scikitlearn.org/stable/modules/generated/sklearn.model_selection.GridSearchCV.html

Twitter Bots' Detection with Benford's Law and Machine Learning

Sanmesh Bhosale and Fabio Di Troia$^{(\boxtimes)}$ (iD)

San José State University, San Jose, CA 95192, USA
fabio.ditroia@sjsu.edu

Abstract. Online Social Networks (OSNs) have grown exponentially in terms of active users and have now become an influential factor in the formation of public opinions. For this reason, the use of bots and botnets for spreading misinformation on OSNs has become a widespread concern. Identifying bots and botnets on Twitter can require complex statistical methods to score a profile based on multiple features. Benford's Law, or the Law of Anomalous Numbers, states that, in any naturally occurring sequence of numbers, the First Significant Leading Digit (FSLD) frequency follows a particular pattern such that they are unevenly distributed and reducing. This principle can be applied to the first-degree egocentric network of a Twitter profile to assess its conformity to such law and, thus, classify it as a bot profile or normal profile. This paper focuses on leveraging Benford's Law in combination with various Machine Learning (ML) classifiers to identify bot profiles on Twitter. In addition, a comparison with other statistical methods is produced to confirm our classification results.

Keywords: Benford's law · Twitter · Machine learning · Social bots · Social networks

1 Introduction

Online Social Networks (OSNs), or Social Media Platforms (SMPs) as we know them, have accumulated millions of users worldwide [20]. With the exponential growth in the number of accounts and active users on OSNs, it is becoming harder and harder to moderate the content and account activities. While a genuine user and malicious user are being considered in this scenario, we also need to consider informational bots and malicious bots. OSNs have been plagued with many types of malicious bots in recent years. Twitter is a popular microblogging and social networking service with millions of users worldwide. Twitter account holders have the option to follow other accounts, and can have any number of accounts following them. Each account can post status updates with a limit of 280 character in the form of "tweets". Twitter has gained popularity due to its adaptation by numerous influential figures and regular political coverage. These services offered by Twitter have become a target of social media bots

L. Bathen et al. (Eds.): SVCC 2022, CCIS 1683, pp. 38–54, 2022.
https://doi.org/10.1007/978-3-031-24049-2_3

for spreading fake and malicious content online. One of the biggest example of bots spreading fake news and malicious misinformation was during the 2016 U.S. presidential election where Russian bots tried to interfere in the election [23]. Since then, Twitter has taken numerous measures for content moderation by suspending suspicious accounts that spread misinformation, and flagging baseless or questionable tweets.

In the context of OSNs, a social bot or a suspicious user account is a computer algorithm or script that automatically interacts with other accounts and produces content without human input or intervention. There are different types of bots, but we only considered two scenarios where either a bot is malicious, that is, it violates the Twitter community guidelines, or it is an informational bot which is not involved in malicious activities. There can also be different levels of bots such as fully automated bots, partially automated bots, and hacked real user accounts for malicious activities.

Bots or suspicious accounts participate in activities that can seriously harm the integrity of online communities. Previously, there have been numerous studies which tackle the social bots on Twitter with the help of machine learning techniques. There are also some real-time Twitter bot detection platforms such as BotOrNot [7]. Due to these efforts to tackle bots, the bot accounts have started changing their patterns and they are now able to better camouflage themselves such that previous methods are not reliable enough anymore to identify them [14]. This paper focuses on identifying these camouflaged bots with the help of the Benford's Law, Machine Learning (ML) classifiers, and Statistical Analysis.

In Sect. 2, we review the background with various approaches and machine learning techniques used in the past for bot detection on Twitter with the help of multiple research papers, journals, and articles. In Sect. 4, we go over the methodology, experimental setup, and datasets used to implement out research. In Sect. 5, we discuss the results and observations of our experiments. In Sect. 6, the conclusion of our work is presented, and possible future scopes of this research are explored with clarification.

2   Background

In this Section, we discuss the background of our work with particular emphasis on the Benford's Law. Moreover, we list the various classification techniques that we trained and tested on the statistics obtained from such law. We also briefly introduce the evaluation methods used. For further information, we invite the reader to the corresponding references.

We experimented using Logistic Regression [25], Naïve Bayes [24], Support Vector Machine [13], Random Forest [3], AdaBoost [22], and Multi-layer Perceptron [19], and evaluated the models with confusion matrix, accuracy, precision, recall, f-measure, and AUC-ROC curve. More details about these evaluation methods can be found in [8]. To validate our classification results we also applied statistical tests such as Pearson's chi-squared test [21], Kolmogorov-Smirnov test [16], and Mean Absolute Deviation (MAD).

2.1 Benford's Law

The Benford's Law, or Newcomb-Benford's Law, states that in any naturally occurring sequence of numbers, the First Significant Leading Digit (FSLD) frequencies follow a particular pattern such that they are unevenly distributed and reducing in nature [2,18]. In 1881, the astrologer Simon Newcomb first observed that the logarithmic tables in the library had their initial pages dirtier and thet were decaying more rapidly than the latter ones [18]. He concluded that the initial digits are more commonly to appear or been used than the latter digits. After 50 years, the physicist Frank Benford re-discovered this lost phenomenon and, later, published a paper titled "The Law of Anomalous Numbers" [2]. For experimentation, he researched on 20 sets of naturally occurring sequences with more than 20,000 samples which included data from sources such as river areas, population, newspapers, addresses, and death rates [2]. All the different datasets tested by him followed the Benford's Law and can be calculated with the formula in Eq. 1, where $P(d)$ is the predicted value for the digit d.

$$P(d) = log_{10}(1 + \frac{1}{d}) \tag{1}$$

However, the Benford's Law does not occur in all datasets. There are certain conditions that a dataset must fulfil to satisfy this property [17]. We list these conditions comparing them with Twitter user accounts information:

- All digits from 1 to 9 should occur in leading position. In our Twitter datasets all digits from 1 to 9 can be possible FSLDs when we consider following_counts.
- There should be a greater occurrence of smaller numbers than larger numbers. In our Twitter datasets, the small numbers are more likely to occur than larger numbers when we consider status_counts.
- The dataset should be natural. Twitter relationships where users follow each other should form organically. There are botnets which will follow a particular user to inflate their followers_counts when paid for the service.
- There should be no sequence in numbers. Every individual Twitter account has different number of status_counts, following_counts, and followers_counts.
- No predefined boundaries. Twitter has no maximum or minimum number set for the parameters such as favorite_counts, likes_counts, and status_counts.
- Different orders of magnitude. Twitter has numbers in tens, hundreds, thousands, and even in millions.
- Dataset should be large. Twitter has millions of users, hence, a large dataset of users is accessible for research.

The experimental findings of Prof. Jennifer Golbeck in [11,12], and Lale Madahali & Margeret Hall in [15], have paved the way for the use of Benford's Law on the first-degree egocentric network of any social media profile for its Benford Analysis. It has been experimentally proved that first significant leading digits of friend counts of a social media account follow the Benford's distribution given in Table 1 [11,12]. If any account does not follow the Benford's distribution, it can be a suspicious account or malicious bot.

Table 1. Benford's distribution FSLD frequencies [2]

Digit	Frequency (%)
1	30.103
2	17.609
3	12.494
4	9.691
5	7.918
6	6.695
7	5.799
8	5.115
9	4.576

3   Related Work

This Section discusses the previous work of social bot detection on Twitter and analyzes the performance and drawbacks of different approaches with and without application of Benford's Law. We also show some of the drawbacks of the previous work which complicates the detection of bots on social media platforms.

Twitter was launched in 2006 as a simple mobile app. However, it quickly grew into a full-fledged communication platform. Most of the previous work tackles the problem of social bot detection with supervised machine learning [6].

An example of machine learning applied to Twitter bot detection is the Botometer service, formerly known as BotOrNot service. This is a popular publicly available bot detection tool which produces a real-time social bot score for Twitter accounts [7]. The BotOrNot service was released in May 2014, and it has been developed by researchers from Indiana University at Bloomington. The service is based on a supervised machine learning classifier which leverages over 1,000 features of the target account to produce a classification score or social bot score. According to its algorithm, the higher is the score the more likely is that target account is being controlled by a software. To obtain a feedback from this tool, the target account's 200 most recent tweets, and 100 recent mentions from other users are required. Its features can be grouped into six main classes, namely, Network, User, Friends, Temporal, Content, and Sentiment. The classifier has been trained on 15,000 manually verified bots, and 16,000 human accounts. The main issue to address is the lack of a standard definition for a social bot. Hence, the labelled datasets used to train the classifier are created by researchers after manual analysis. This technique can introduce bias due to human error. Botometer is accessible through both a web interface and an API endpoint.

The researchers Chu et al. have designed a supervised machine learning classifier to distinguish a target account into three different groups, that is, human, bot, and cyborg [5]. An account classified as human is defined as to have no automated activity, whereas an account classified as bot is fully automated. An account with a mix of automated and non-automated activity is classified as a cyborg. Their classifier is based on four components, namely, entropy, machine learning, account properties, and decision maker. The entropy component is used to recognize automation by detecting a periodic timing for tweeting. The machine learning component is based on a Bayesian classifier to identify text patterns of social spambots on Twitter. The account properties component analyses account information to differentiate humans from bots. Finally, the decision maker component employs Linear Discriminant Analysis on the features shortlisted by other three components to make a classification. The researchers collected their data by crawling on Twitter using the Twitter API, and found that their dataset constitutes of 53% human, 36% cyborg, and 11% bot accounts. The researchers have used a very small dataset for the training of the classifier, and have changed a binary classification problem into multi-class classification problem by introducing cyborgs. As the results in Fig. 1 show, their classifier is effective in identifying humans and bots apart but is less confident when classifying between human and cyborg accounts, or bot and cyborg accounts.

		Classified			Total	True Pos.%
		Human	Cyborg	Bot		
	Human	949	51	0	1000	94.90%
Actual	Cyborg	98	828	74	1000	82.80%
	Bot	0	63	937	1000	93.70%

Fig. 1. Confusion matrix on human, cyborg, and bot classification [5].

In 2015, Dr. Jennifer Golbeck from University of Maryland College Park was the first to apply Benford's Law on the data from OSNs [12]. The author experimented with five major OSNs, namely, Facebook, Google Plus, LiveJournal, Pinterest, and Twitter. They were able to discover that certain features of OSNs, such as the friend's following_counts, conformed to Benford's Law , that is, Benford's Law was applicable to the first-degree egocentric networks of a target profile. Figure 2 shows those statistics. Specifically, the research findings on Twitter dataset indicate that accounts which strongly deviated from Benford's Law were engaged in malicious or unnatural behavior. The Twitter dataset used for analysis of the Benford's Law has been made public by the author [10].

This discovery from [12] led the author to test the hypothesis that the social connections made by bots are unnatural in nature and they tend to violate Benford's Law [11]. The author re-investigated the previously discovered Russian bot accounts from 2015, and uncovered a larger Russian botnet with about 13,609 Twitter accounts, out of which 99.6 percent did not conform to Benford's Law.

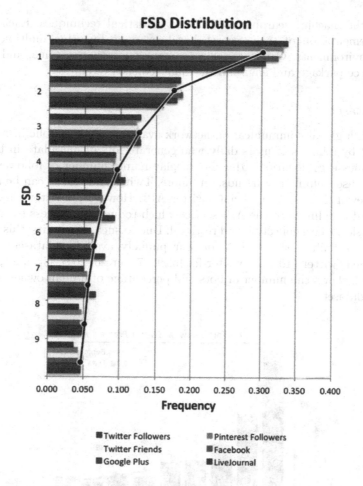

Fig. 2. FSLDs for Twitter, Google Plus, Pinterest, Facebook [12].

This study concluded that first significant leading digits of a friend's follow-ing counts can be utilized to identify anomalous behavior of malicious bots, and it is a significant feature to differentiate between humans and malicious bots. Unfortunately, the author has not made the Russian botnet dataset used in this research public.

In this research, we continue the previous work by combining the promis-ing results of Benford's Law applied to Twitter bot detection to the theory of machine learning.

4   Implementation

In this Section, we discuss in detail the database and step-by-step pipeline for the implementation of this research. This Section explains the setup followed to train the machine learning models and statistical techniques. Each part of the implementation of this research has been done by using multiple Conda virtual environments. Conda can run on many operating systems, and it is an open-source package and environment management system [1].

4.1 Dataset

Twitter is a global communication network available to the public in real-time. It is used by millions of users daily who generate lots of metadata in the form of short messages, location, @handle, display name, number of followers, number of statuses, number of friends, and more. Twitter metadata can be accessed and retrieved through the official Twitter API. However, Twitter has recently announced rate limits to the API service which reduces the access to the metadata and slows data collection and retrieval. Due to such rate limits, this research dataset was built with the help of four publicly available datasets, namely, anonymizedTwitter [10], botometer-feedback [7], cresci-2017 [6], and gilani-17 [9]. Table 2 shows the number of bots and percentage of human owned accounts for each datasets.

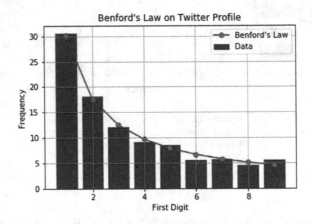

Fig. 3. anonymizedTwitter data samples following Benford's Law Distribution.

4.2 Approach

The approach that we implemented is divided into two easy steps, that is, first, preprocessing each dataset and combining them, then, training and testing multiple classifier models and selecting the best model. An overview of our approach is given in Fig. 5 with the application of MLP. We collected the following counts of all the friends of the profile under scrutiny and extracted the FSLD frequencies to feed our neural network classifier. The input to the models is fixed in size and is equal to 9, that is, every input is the frequency of that particular first significant leading digit. Before outputting the result, the prediction is compared

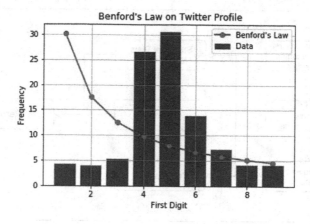

Fig. 4. anonymizedTwitter data samples not following Benford's Law Distribution.

Table 2. Datasets bot and human label counts

Dataset	Bots	Humans (%)
anonymizedTwitter	317	20,818
botometer-feedback	143	372
cresci-2017	9391	3474
gilani-17	1,090	1,413
Total	10,941	26,077

with the majority vote of our statistical tests. This step is necessary only to prove the efficacy of our technique.

4.3   Data Preprocessing

Since the first dataset, anonymizedTwitter, did not have labels, labelling was performed. Specifically, the FSLDs of each of the 21,135 data samples were extracted from their following_counts and then their frequencies were visualized in the form of a histogram against the Benford's Law distribution, one sample at a time. Exploratory data analysis was performed on each data sample and a bot or human label was assigned to all samples.

The datasets from [6,9,26] were only used to collect the Twitter @handle and the 'bot' or 'human' label provided by the original authors. Afterwards, the first-degree egocentric network data, that is, the following_counts of each friend for that @handle, was collected with the help of the Twitter API. Once all the first-degree egocentric data from each of the four datasets was available, a new combined dataset was created. This combined dataset only contained the FSLD frequencies of each data sample and a label of 0 for human accounts and 1 for bot profiles. Figure 3 shows the congruity of the anonymizedTwitter dataset

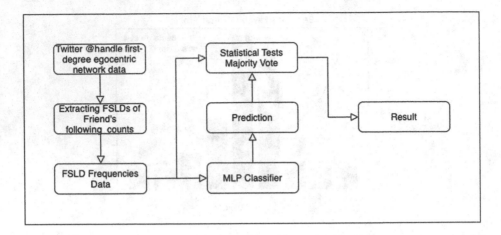

Fig. 5. Overview of our approach.

samples to the Benford's Law Distribution (legitimate users), while Fig. 4 shows the samples that are not following such law (possible bots). Figure 6, instead, shows the FSLD frequencies for few samples (one per row) selected from our combined dataset, three bots (label 1) and two human accounts (label 0). It is possible to notice how the rows with bot label 1 are not following the Benford's Law distribution.

1	2	3	4	5	6	7	8	9	Bot
0.00	100.00	0.00	0.00	0.00	0.00	0.00	0.00	0.00	1
31.82	19.48	7.79	11.04	7.14	7.14	4.55	3.90	7.14	0
2.11	96.43	0.70	0.13	0.13	0.06	0.13	0.13	0.19	1
40.00	16.36	11.82	5.45	4.55	9.09	6.36	3.64	2.73	0
18.57	5.02	24.19	2.05	1.15	1.51	11.23	18.81	17.45	1

Fig. 6. Final dataset with FSLD frequencies and bot label.

4.4 Training and Testing Classifiers

Once the preprocessing was completed and the combined dataset with labels was available, the data was split into train and test sets with a 75:25 split. Synthetic Minority Oversampling Technique (SMOTE) [4] was used to treat the imbalance between our bot and human samples. We trained and tested six supervised machine learning classifiers, namely, Logistic Regression, Naïve Bayes, Support Vector Machine, Random Forest, AdaBoost, and Multi-layer Perceptron. Random Forest and AdaBoost models gave high accuracy scores, but the best model was the Multi-layer Perceptron.

5   Results

In this Section, we discuss the results of the experiments performed in our research. The training results for each machine learning model are discussed in detail. The summary of all the experiments' results are given in Table 3.

Table 3. Naïve Bayes performance

Model	Accuracy	Precision	Recall	F-Measure
Naive Bayes	95.44%	99.02%	89.68%	94.12%
Logistic regression	99.11%	98.59%	99.22%	98.91%
SVC	99.82%	99.56%	100%	99.78%
Random forest	99.91%	99.83%	99.95%	99.89%
AdaBoost classifier	99.93%	99.89%	99.95%	99.92%
MLP	99.98%	100%	99.95%	99.97%

5.1   Naïve Bayes

The first phase of experiments was the training and testing of Naïve Bayes classifier. This was a naïve approach as the model considers all the features independently with no correlation. With all the nine features evaluated independently the Naïve bayes model obtain detection accuracy of 95.44%, precision of 99.02%, recall of 89.68%, and f-measure of 94.12%. Figure 7 shows the AUC-ROC curve and Confusion Matrix.

5.2   Logistic Regression

In the second phase of experiments, we trained the logistic regression model. Since we have only nine features, we obtained detection accuracy of 99.11%, precision of 98.59%, recall of 99.22%, and f-measure of 98.91%. Figure 8 shows the AUC-ROC curve and Confusion Matrix.

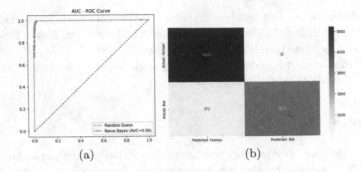

Fig. 7. AUC-ROC curve (a) and Confusion Matrix (b) of Naïve Bayes

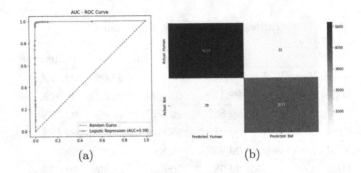

Fig. 8. AUC-ROC curve (a) and Confusion Matrix (b) of Logistic Regression

5.3 SVM

In the third phase of experiments, we trained and tested a Support Vector Machine (SVM) model on our dataset. The SVM took more time to train that the previous experiments, but it is well suited for our dataset as we have a binary classification problem at hand. We obtained a detection accuracy of 99.82%, precision of 99.56%, recall of 100.00%, and f-measure of 99.78%. Figure 9 shows the AUC-ROC curve and Confusion Matrix.

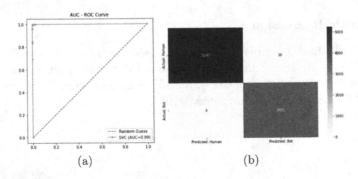

Fig. 9. AUC-ROC curve (a) and Confusion Matrix (b) of Support Vector Machine

5.4   Random Forest

In the fourth phase of experiments, we trained and tested a Random Forest classifier which uses multiple decision trees to gain high accuracy. The model trained faster that SVM and has better overall performance compared to all the previous tests. We obtained detection accuracy of 99.91%, precision of 99.83%, recall of 99.95%, and f-measure of 99.89%. Figure 10 shows the AUC-ROC curve and Confusion Matrix.

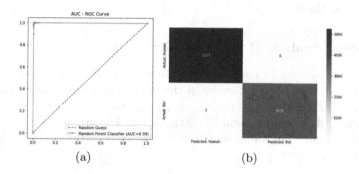

Fig. 10. AUC-ROC curve (a) and Confusion Matrix (b) of Random Forest

5.5   AdaBoost

The fifth phase of experiments was to push the accuracy score as high as possible, thus, we trained and tested an Adaptive Boosting model. This is another ensemble learning technique, such as Random Forest, that obtained detection accuracy of 99.93%, precision of 99.89%, recall of 99.95%, and f-measure of 99.92%. Figure 11 shows the AUC-ROC curve and Confusion Matrix.

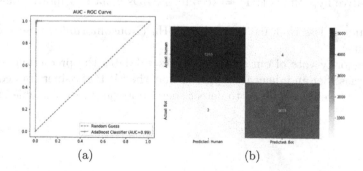

Fig. 11. AUC-ROC curve (a) and Confusion Matrix (b) of AdaBoost Classifier

5.6   Multi-layer Perceptron

The sixth and final phase of experiments was completed by training and testing a feedforward neural network model called Multi-layer Perceptron (MLP). The MLP classifier have an Input and Output layer just like the Logistic Regression model, but it also has hidden layers with neurons to achieve the best possible results. The MLP model obtained the highest accuracy (near perfect) and overall performance. We obtained detection accuracy of 99.98%, precision of 100.00%, recall of 99.95%, and f-measure of 99.97%. Figure 12 shows the AUC-ROC curve and Confusion Matrix.

5.7   Latency Analysis of ML Algorithms

We studied the latency in training our supervised machine learning models on our combined dataset. When the size of the dataset increases, the training time of our models tended also to increase significantly. We trained each of our models on our training dataset of around 25,000 samples. The latency analysis is based on the training time (in milliseconds) taken by each model. Table 4 shows our latency analysis results.

5.8   Statistical Tests Majority Vote

Once the MLP model was trained and selected for its high-performance accuracy, we were ready to test our model on new accounts and then verify our model's classification based on a majority vote of our three statistical tests. We took four random samples with two bots and two humans and tested our MLP classifier prediction with our statistical tests for majority vote. Here we are testing the goodness of fit of the FSLDs with the Benford's Law distribution. The hypothesis for tests was formulated as:

Null hypothesis (H0) = Account FSLDs follow Benford's Law
Alternative hypothesis (H1) = Account FSLDs violate Benford's Law

If p-value is less than 0.05, then reject H_0 (Nonconformity), else accept H_0 (Conformity)

The majority vote of our statistical tests validates the prediction results of our MLP classifier and, hence, we proved that the MLP classifier trained on our combined dataset can be used to detect social bots on Twitter (Table 5).

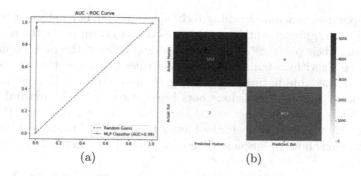

Fig. 12. AUC-ROC curve (a) and Confusion Matrix (b) of Multi-layer Perceptron

Table 4. Latency analysis on training dataset

Model	Latency (ms)
Naïve Bayes	7.26
Logistic regression	51.26
Support vector machine	2935.64
Random forest classifier	1862.07
AdaBoost classifier	1526.95
Multi-layer perceptron	3308.19

Table 5. Statistical tests majority vote

Test	Bot1	Bot2	Human1	Human2
Pearson Chi-Squared	Nonconformity	Nonconformity	Conformity	Conformity
Kolmogorov-Smirnov	Nonconformity	Conformity	Conformity	Conformity
Pearson Correlation Coeff	Nonconformity	Nonconformity	Conformity	Conformity
Majority vote	**Bot**	**Bot**	**Human**	**Human**

6   Conclusions and Future Works

The proposed technique, which collects the following counts of all the friends of the profile under scrutiny and extract the FSLD frequencies to feed our neural network classifier, works best for classifying malicious social bots from human accounts. This is due to the strategic selection of our databases used as ground truth for training our model. The main goal of our research was to create a ground truth dataset from scratch and to train a neural network model on the dataset, while also validating the results with majority vote of statistical tests. The research enables us to identify if a Twitter user is a malicious social bot or human with high level of confidence. The overall research technique is novel, and has never been implemented in this fashion as far as the authors are aware.

Any supervised machine learning technique used for bot detection will only be as good as the ground truth data that was used to train it. As the social bots keep changing their patterns and techniques rapidly, even the most sophisticate bot detection algorithms fail as their training rules become outdated. Benford's Law is an unavoidable naturally occurring phenomenon and it is prevalent on Twitter's data. Since the malicious bots break away from the natural pattern by synthetically following other social bots and malicious accounts, they tend to unknowingly violate the Benford's Law. Hence, our technique will be able to identify malicious bots or suspicious accounts even if the bot behavior patterns keep evolving.

However, there are certain limitations to take in considerations. To analyze any account on Twitter, we need the account to be following at least 100 other accounts. The detection accuracy, in fact, deteriorates if the account has less friends. Furthermore, Benford's Law requires orders of magnitude and certain number of samples to work with the FSLD frequency distribution.

6.1 Future Works

The research can be extended to create a web browser plug-in where the users is able to classify Twitter accounts in real-time without gathering all the first-degree egocentric data and feeding it to our model. The browser extension could be able to add graphical and textual information on the Twitter page to warn the user about any suspicious profile that is encountered during regular activity.

Another extension to this research would be the employment of other techniques to identify if the suspicious account is part of a bigger botnet.

This same technique can also be applied on Facebook datasets, or other social media platforms, to test if we can successfully classify bots on such platform with the help of the Benford's Law.

References

1. Anaconda, I.: Conda (2017). https://docs.conda.io/. Accessed 11 Nov 2012
2. Benford, F.: The law of anomalous numbers. Proc. Am. Philos. Soc. **78**, 551–572 (1938)
3. Breiman, L.: Random forests. Mach. Learn. **45**(1), 5–32 (2001). https://doi.org/10.1023/a:1010933404324
4. Chawla, N.V., Bowyer, K.W., Hall, L.O., Kegelmeyer, W.P.: SMOTE: synthetic minority over-sampling technique. J. Artif. Intel. Res. **16**, 321–357 (2002)
5. Chu, Z., Gianvecchio, S., Wang, H., Jajodia, S.: Who is tweeting on Twitter: human, bot, or cyborg? In: Proceedings of the 26th Annual Computer Security Applications Conference, pp. 21–30 (2010)
6. Cresci, S., Di Pietro, R., Petrocchi, M., Spognardi, A., Tesconi, M.: The paradigm-shift of social spambots: evidence, theories, and tools for the arms race. In: Proceedings of the 26th International Conference on World Wide Web Companion, pp. 963–972 (2017)

7. Davis, C.A., Varol, O., Ferrara, E., Flammini, A., Menczer, F.: BotOrNot: a system to evaluate social bots. In: Proceedings of the 25th International Conference Companion on World Wide Web, pp. 273–274 (2016)
8. Davis, J., Goadrich, M.: The relationship between Precision-Recall and ROC curves. In: Proceedings of the 23rd International Conference on Machine Learning, pp. 233–240 (2006)
9. Gilani, Z., Farahbakhsh, R., Tyson, G., Wang, L., Crowcroft, J.: Of bots and humans (on Twitter). In: Proceedings of the 2017 IEEE/ACM International Conference on Advances in Social Networks Analysis and Mining, pp. 349–354 (2017)
10. Golbeck, J.: Benford data (2015). https://github.com/jgolbeck/BenfordData. Accessed 23 June 2022
11. Golbeck, J.: Benford's law applies to online social networks. PLoS ONE **10**(8), e0135169 (2015)
12. Golbeck, J.: Benford's law can detect malicious social bots. First Monday **24**, 8 (2019)
13. Hearst, M.A., Dumais, S.T., Osuna, E., Platt, J., Scholkopf, B.: Support vector machines. IEEE Intel. Syst. Appl. **13**(4), 18–28 (1998)
14. Kolomeets, M., Tushkanova, O., Levshun, D., Chechulin, A.: Camouflaged bot detection using the friend list. In: 2021 29th Euromicro International Conference on Parallel, Distributed and Network-Based Processing (PDP), pp. 253–259. IEEE (2021)
15. Madahali, L., Hall, M.: Application of the benford's law to social bots and information operations activities. In: 2020 International Conference on Cyber Situational Awareness, Data Analytics and Assessment (CyberSA), pp. 1–8. IEEE (2020)
16. Massey, F.J., Jr.: The Kolmogorov-Smirnov test for goodness of fit. J. Am. Stat. Assoc. **46**(253), 68–78 (1951)
17. Mbona, I., Eloff, J.H.: Feature selection using benford's law to support detection of malicious social media bots. Inf. Sci. **582**, 369–381 (2022)
18. Newcomb, S.: Note on the frequency of use of the different digits in natural numbers. Am. J. Math. **4**(1), 39–40 (1881)
19. Noriega, L.: Multilayer perceptron tutorial. School of Computing. Staffordshire University (2005)
20. Ortiz-Ospina, E.: Our world in data (2019). https://ourworldindata.org/rise-of-social-media. Accessed 23 June 2022
21. Plackett, R.L.: Karl Pearson and the chi-squared test. Int. Stat. Rev. Int. Stat. **51**, 59–72 (1983)
22. Schapire, Robert E..: Explaining AdaBoost. In: Schölkopf, Bernhard, Luo, Zhiyuan, Vovk, Vladimir (eds.) Empirical Inference, pp. 37–52. Springer, Heidelberg (2013). https://doi.org/10.1007/978-3-642-41136-6_5
23. Time.com: Here's what we know so far about Russia's 2016 meddling (2019). https://time.com/5565991/russia-influence-2016-election/. Accessed 11 Nov 2012
24. Webb, G.I., Keogh, E., Miikkulainen, R.: Naïve Bayes. Encycl. Mach. Learn. **15**, 713–714 (2010)
25. Wright, R.E.: Logistic regression (1995)
26. Yang, K.C., Varol, O., Davis, C.A., Ferrara, E., Flammini, A., Menczer, F.: Arming the public with artificial intelligence to counter social bots. Human Behav. Emerg. Technol. **1**(1), 48–61 (2019)

Blockchain and Smart Contracts

A Blockchain-Based Retribution Mechanism for Collaborative Intrusion Detection

Wenjun Fan[1,4], Shubham Kumar[2], Sang-Yoon Chang[3,4], and Younghee Park[2,4](✉)

[1] School of Advanced Technology, Xi'an Jiaotong-Liverpool University, Suzhou 215123, Jiangsu,
People's Republic of China
wenjun.fan@xjtlu.edu.cn
[2] Computer Engineering Department, San José State University, San José, CA 95192, USA
{shubham.kumar,younghee.park}@sjsu.edu
[3] Department of Computer Science, College of Engineering and Applied Science, University of Colorado Colorado Springs, Colorado Springs, CO 80918, USA
schang2@uccs.edu
[4] Silicon Valley Cybersecurity Institute (SVCSI), San José, CR 95192, USA

Abstract. Collaborative intrusion detection approach uses the shared detection signature between the collaborative participants to facilitate coordinated defense. In the context of collaborative intrusion detection system (CIDS), however, there is no research focusing on the efficiency of the shared detection signature. The inefficient detection signature costs not only the IDS resource but also the process of the peer-to-peer (P2P) network. In this paper, we therefore propose a blockchain-based retribution mechanism, which aims to incentivize the participants to contribute to verifying the efficiency of the detection signature in terms of certain distributed consensus. We implement a prototype using Ethereum blockchain, which instantiates a token-based retribution mechanism and a smart contract-enabled voting-based distributed consensus. We conduct a number of experiments built on the prototype, and the experimental results demonstrate the effectiveness of the proposed approach.

Keywords: Blockchain · Collaborative intrusion detection · Retribution · Detection signature · Verification · Token

1 Introduction

A collaborative intrusion detection system (CIDS) [17] can share security information (e.g., the intrusion signature) across multiple domains to gain a collaborative intelligence for intrusion detection. A CIDS can have a global view for large networks or IT ecosystems in contrast to the standalone IDS that only monitors the intrusion events occurring at one place. In the context of CIDS,

© The Author(s) 2022
L. Bathen et al. (Eds.): SVCC 2022, CCIS 1683, pp. 57–73, 2022.
https://doi.org/10.1007/978-3-031-24049-2_4

there are two architectures [18]: centralized and distributed. A centralized CIDS often applies a centralized server to collect and share the security information to the distributed IDS, and such a centralized server is often deployed in cloud [5,7]. However, the centralized server often suffers the single point of failure, and the cloud is also honest-but-curious. On the contrary, a distributed CIDS relies on a peer-to-peer (P2P) network to propagate the security information. However, the distributed CIDS has to cope with other security problems, e.g., it needs to ensure the integrity of the data transmission and to build the trust among the participants. For addressing those issues, several blockchain-based CIDSes have been proposed [6,11,13,16].

The blockchain-based CIDSes often use permissioned blockchain, which means any participant must be registered to the authority which could be a centralized CA [11,16] or a distributed PKI [6]. Also, one blockchain-based CIDS often involves distributed consensus protocol to verify and agree the propagated viable transmissions. Most consensuses of the CIDSes focus on resisting against the insider attacks, e.g., a number of participants collude together (or are controlled by the attacker) to issue/verify the malicious transmissions across the whole P2P network. To address this, the blockchain P2P network can use practical Byzantine Fault Tolerance (pBFT)-based voting to achieve the n-compromise resistance [6]. However, this research area lacks an approach to verify the efficiency of the shared detection signature.

A *detection signature* is a malicious data pattern or attack rule that is compared with current behavior to decide if is that of an intruder. The unverified but widely adopted detection signature not only costs the CIDS resource but also impacts the coordinated defense, because some participants may yield false alerts due to the incorrect/inefficient detection signature.

In this paper, we propose a blockchain-based retribution mechanism to verify the propagated detection signature for CIDS. The following properties of the blockchain typically motivate our approach: i) *decentralization* includes distinct autonomous participants which is consistent with the nature of the CIDS; ii) *digital currency* provides the financial nature to incentivize the participants to contribute to donating and verifying detection signatures; iii) *consensus* enables the participants of the P2P network to reach agreement based on a distributed manner; iv) *smart contract* provides the programmability to create specific consensus for processing certain payload of transaction; v) *permissioned blockchain* controls the participation of the blockchain network.

The retribution mechanism aims to reward the participants who donate efficient detection signatures and punish the participants who share inefficient detection signatures. Thus, the retribution mechanism introduces an incentive to the participants to take part in the coordinated defense by sharing efficient detection signatures. The contributions of this paper are summarized as follows:

- A blockchain-based retribution mechanism is proposed, which is used for incentivizing the participants to contribute to the collaborative intrusion detection system.

- An Ethereum blockchain-based prototype is implemented for validating the approach, whereby the Ethereum token is applied as the incentive.
- The corresponding experiments are conducted to show the effectiveness of the proposed approach.

The rest of the paper is organized as follows: Sect. 2 reviews the related work; Sect. 3 presents our models including the system network model and the threat model that our approach builds on; Sect. 4 proposes the design of the blockchain-based retribution mechanism; Sect. 5 presents the Ethereum blockchain-based prototype implementation; Sect. 6 shows the experimental results; Sect. 7 concludes the paper.

2 Related Work

In this section, we review the related work including the existing retribution mechanisms in the context of blockchain P2P network and the detection signature verification methods in the IDS research area.

2.1 Retribution Mechanism

The well-known retribution mechanism in the context of Blockchain P2P network is IKP [12], which provides an instant Karma mechanism to the distributed PKI based on permissionless cryptocurrency blockchain. The major contribution of IKP is that it proposes a resilient mechanism to provide incentives to the CAs to perform correctly and to the detectors to report unauthorized certificates. IKP is used to detect the unauthorized certificates for a domain due to CA misbehavior in terms of certificate policies that specify automatic responses. However, IKP still involves the mining process which is consistent with Nakamoto consensus provides natural financial incentives for the participants in the permissionless blockchain P2P network, in contrast to that, our approach is used for the permissioned blockchain without mining process.

Apart from monetary incentive based retribution mechanism, some other approaches consider using reputation to reward or punish the participants. Thus, we also consider the Proof-of-Reputation (PoR) as related work where the reputation serves as incentive to push the nodes to participate in the distributed consensus [8,14,19]. PoR is used to replace the Proof-of-Work (PoW) consensus essentially to reduce the heavy computation power requirement and increase the scalability of the blockchain P2P network, while PoR itself should resist against the attacker whose objective is to get high reputation. The PoR-based consensus often allows the node having the highest reputation to sign the block, or uses the reputation to weight the vote of the node. That is different from our approach, as we encourage every node to share the new detection signature, and also the reputation is not used to weight the node's vote.

2.2 Detection Signature Verification

There are a number of solutions and research about verifying the detection signature in order to reduce the false positive in the context of signature-based NIDS, e.g., to track and analyze the protocol status code of the response to see if it is valid or unexpected [10]; to use the context knowledge, i.e., the protected network and system configuration to verify the alters [4]; to correlate IDS alarm with network vulnerability [15] using vulnerability scanning tool like Nessus [1]. Another case in point is the challenge-based approach, which evaluates a node's detection correctness by sending challenges and receiving the corresponding feedback [11]. In particular, ATLANTIDES [3] is a notable approach that uses an automatic anomaly-based analysis of the system output, which provides useful context information regarding the network services. In other words, it takes an approach by correlating the anomalies detected on the output with the alerts raised by the NIDS monitoring the input traffic, and built on that, it can discard a number of the latter as being false positive alerts. More specifically, a communication's incoming traffic triggers the signature-based NIDS's alarm, and then ATLANTIDES uses anomaly-based IDS to monitor the outgoing traffic of that communication. If the anomaly-based IDS against outgoing traffic alarms, that is a true positive detection signature, otherwise, that is a false positive one.

All the above approaches focus on verifying the truthfulness of the detection signature, while out work stresses on the efficiency of the detection signature.

3   Models

This section presents the models that our approach is based on, which includes the system network model and the threat model respectively.

3.1 System Network Model

In our approach, the P2P network is decentralized with collaborative detection communication to gain a coordinated defense. We define the (virtual) network boundary that comprises standalone intrusion detection engine nodes across geographical domains. Thus, the system network boundary can be considered as one autonomous system (AS) overseeing multiple domains, or as a single-domain with multiple networking inbound points, e.g., firewalls or security-enabled controllers in SDN network [6]. With this definition, we assume that there is no outsider attacks threatening the coordination communication between the participants, e.g., the Denial-of-Service (DoS) attack making the node unable to participate the distributed consensus [9]. Therefore, we focus on the insider attacks which compromise the participants to share bogus information and manipulate the consensus. Those participants will comprise a permissioned blockchain P2P network, and once such a network is created, the set of peers is static within the defined network boundary.

3.2   Threat Model

The threat model stresses on the insider attacks rather than the outsider attack corresponding to the system network model mentioned above. Hence, the DoS attack from outside against the availability of the participant nodes is out of the scope. Also, we do not consider the insider-and-outsider collusion case, whereby an insider adversary does not share newly discovered detection signature to other participants while inform the zero-day vulnerability to the outsider adversary so that the outsider adversary can exploit the vulnerability.

The objective of an insider adversary is to take malicious actions to disrupt the coordinated defense. More specifically, the insider adversary aims to deliver inefficient detection signatures across the P2P network to enforce other participants to download the inefficient detection signature to update their detection rule set ineffectively. Except for the single node's bad actions, the insider attack often involves the network-wide compromise to manipulate the consensus. That means the adversary has compromised enough participants and can mislead the entire system to make a wrong decision.

The following items are the potential attack vectors that an insider adversary can leverage, which our approach is designed to defend against:

1. **Flooding**: A peer keeps sending tremendous malicious/inefficient detection signatures to other peers to waste their computation resource.
2. **Malicious injection**: A peer submits a malicious/inefficient detection signature to the other coordinated peers, which increases the false alert ratio.
3. **Collusive verification**: Multiple peers collude together to manipulate the distributed consensus to affect the verification result. The objectives of this vector can be i) to share and verify a malicious/inefficient detection signature (*collusive injection*); ii) or to defame a valid/efficient detection signature (*collusive defamation*).

4   Design

This section proposes the system architecture overview, the efficiency calculation method, the distributed verification consensus, and the retribution mechanism as follows.

4.1   System Architecture Overview

An overview of the system architecture is presented by Fig. 1. In our approach, the blockchain is permissioned, and a registered peer can play two alternative roles, *donor* or *verifier*. Also, according to our system network model mentioned in Sect. 3.1, the donor and verifiers can monitor different domains/networks.

When the peer is a donor, it submits detection signature to the P2P network; as a verifier, the peer needs to verify the received detection signature to report the verification result to indicate the efficiency of the detection signature. With

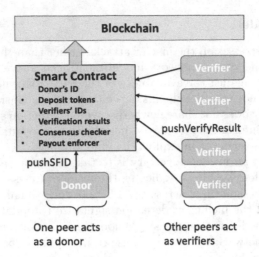

Fig. 1. An overview of the architecture design: it includes n peers; when 1 peer plays as a donor, the rest of the peers play as verifiers.

that, for each detection signature transmitted, there must be a donor and the rest peers become verifiers in nature. We define the efficiency of a detection signature as the presence of the detection signature across the verifiers. If a donor circulates a detection signature, the other peers as verifiers need to examine the presence of the detection signature separately. That means each verifier checks its local rule-sets to see if the examined detection signature exists or not. Thus, if a detection signature presents more times across the peers, it has the higher efficiency. We propose a retribution mechanism (see Sect. 4.4) to incentivize the peers to contribute to verifying the efficiency of the detection signature.

In Fig. 1, assuming there are five peers in the blockchain P2P network, when one of them acts as a donor to push a detection signature file ID (SFID), other peers will play as the verifiers to download and verify the new detection signature separately. It is worth noticing that in practice, people do not directly submit the detection signature file to the blockchain, since storing big size file (like the detection signature file) in blockchain ledger is not economical. Thus, we employ the InterPlanetary File System (IPFS) [2] to store the raw detection signature file, whereby a SFID will be given by IPFS. Thus, the donor just submits the SFID representing the corresponding detection signature to the blockchain, and the verifiers can use the SFID to request to the IPFS for downloading the detection signature for verification.

The distributed verification carried out by multiple verifilers is asynchronous, since every domain has its own context. When a verifier gets a verification result, it needs to report the result to the smart contract. Meanwhile, the consensus checker of the smart contract keeps track of the reports from the verifiers. Once the results achieve a consensus threshold, the smart contract can make the consensus decision and execute the payout enforcer to perform the retribution.

4.2   Efficiency Calculation Method

The verification method is that the verifier examines the presences of the down-loaded detection signature in its own rule set (assuming one presence denotes that the verifier convinces itself that the detection signature is valid by certain checking approach like [3,4,15]). Thus, we define the peer/participant as p, the rule set of p_i as $\mathcal{R}_i$, where $i \in \{1, 2, ..., 3n + 1\}$ (when $3n + 1$ is the total number of the peers participating in the P2P network to support the n-compromise resistance), the detection signature as s, the count of the presence of s in $\mathcal{R}_i$ as $x_i \in \mathcal{Z}$. Thus, if $s \notin \mathcal{R}_i$, $x_i = 0$; if $s \in \mathcal{R}_i$, $x_i \geqslant 1$. Also, we define the total number of the rules in $\mathcal{R}_i$ as y_i, and the efficiency of s calculated by p_i as f_{s_i}. Thus, f_{s_i} can be calculated by the following Eq. (1):

$$f_{s_i} = \frac{x_i}{y_i} \times 100\% \tag{1}$$

All the verifiers need to report the efficiency of s from their own perspectives respectively to the smart contract. If $f_{s_i} \geqslant 50\%$, the smart contract considers that s is efficient for p_i; whereas if $f_{s_i} < 50\%$, the smart contract considers that s is inefficient for p_i. The smart contract counts the number of p who reports the efficiency of s which is greater than or equal to 50%, meanwhile, counts the number of p who reports the efficiency of s which is less than 50%. These two counted numbers will be used to make an unanimous decision based on a distributed consensus (see Sect. 4.3) as an overall verification result to s.

4.3   Distributed Verification Consensus

The distributed verification consensus presented here is used to ensure the distributed verification of the efficiency of the propagated detection signature, which is different from the distributed consensus used for mining the block in permissionless cryptocurrency. Hence, we use the practical Byzantine Fault Tolerance (pBFT)-based voting to sustain the distributed verification consensus, which provides an "n-compromise resistance" against the up to n participants compromise where we have $3n + 1$ participants in total. In other words, our distributed verification consensus is based on a majority decision, whereby even 1/3 of the participants are compromised to perform collusive verification to make an inefficient s become efficient, the whole P2P network can still work and resist against such an insider attack.

It is worth noting that Ethereum itself does not use pBFT as the consensus algorithm for processing the transactions/blocks, while we use pBFT with smart contract just for voting (and verifying) for the detection signature file proposed by any peer. With using the pBFT-based voting for the distributed verification consensus, the smart contract only makes the unanimous decision saying that s is efficient when more than 2/3 of the total participants reporting that s is efficient. Otherwise, s is judged as inefficient. Thus, our system is strict to decide an efficient s (i.e., must have more than 2/3 participants agree) while is loose to decide an inefficient s (i.e., only needs at least 1/3 participants agree).

Table 1. Operations of the retribution scheme vs. the threats.

Operation	Threat
Deposit (donor)	Flooding
Penalty (donor)	Malicious injection
Reward (donor)	Malicious injection
Reward (verifiers)	Collusive verification

In addition, once the consensus is done, there must be a majority group and a minority group, unless the number of participants agreeing on the efficiency of s equals the number of participants agreeing on the inefficiency of s. We define the total number of verifiers which report result as n_v, the number of the majority verifiers as n_{major} and the number of the minority verifiers as n_{minor}. Thus, $n_v = n_{major} + n_{minor}$. In the event that s is efficient, the majority group must includes the participants supporting the efficiency of s, and the minority group must consist of the participants reporting the inefficiency of s. In contrast, if s is verified as an inefficient one, the majority group and the minority group could include either kind of participants respectively, i.e., the majority group could be comprised of the participants supporting the inefficiency of s while the minority group could consist of the participants supporting the efficiency of s, or vice versa.

4.4 Retribution Mechanism

The retribution mechanism represents the reward and punishment methods incentivizing the participants to contribute to donating and verifying the detection signature. To this end, we define three sorts of token-based operations: *deposit, penalty* and *reward*. Table 1 summarizes these operations with the threats (mentioned in Sect. 3.2) resisted against. These operations are detailed as follows.

Deposit. The deposit operation indicates that one donor must deposit a number of tokens accompany with the submission of s. We define the number of the deposited tokens as d. Such an operation can effectively prevent the submission flooding launched by the malicious donor, as now any donor has to deposit a certain number of tokens for submission, meaning the submission is not free.

Penalty. The penalty operation towards the donor means that if the submitted s turns out to be inefficient based on the consensus result reported by the verifiers, then d will be deducted completely. Such as operation can effectively mitigate the malicious injection including inefficient s, since if the submitted s is inefficient, the deposit will be deducted as a penalty to the donor.

Reward (donor). The reward operation towards the donor denotes that if the submitted s is verified as an efficient one, the donor will get the deposit back and also get a number of extra tokens as reward for its contribution. We define the number of the reward tokens for the donor as r_d. In our case, we specify $r_d = d$, which means the donor will get $2d$ back as reward, and that actually awards the donor the number of tokens for one extra submission attempt. Such an operation can incentivize the donor to submit efficient s in order to get the deposit and the extra reward back.

Reward (verifier). Regarding the reward for the verifiers, we define the verifier as v_i where $i \in \{1, 2, ...3n\}$ (as there is one out of the $3n + 1$ participants already playing as a donor), the number of the reward tokens for all the verifiers as r_v, which equals the number of the deposited tokens from the donor, i.e., $r_v = d$. If the verifier belongs to the majority group, it will get a maximized reward, defined as r_{v-max}, and if the verifier belongs to the minority group, it will get a minimized reward, defined as r_{v-min}. Note that $r_v = r_{v-max} + r_{v-min}$. In addition, if $n_{major} = n_{minor}$, r_v will be divided by n_v, which then is allocated to every v_i equally, though this kind of event occurs occasionally. With that, we define the reward per majority verifier as $r_{per-major}$, the reward per minority verifier as $r_{per-minor}$, and the reward per verifier as r_{per-v} (when $n_{major} = n_{minor}$). Such an operation can incentivize the verifiers to report their verification results, and also can resist against the collusive verification when the malicious verifiers intend to make an inefficient s become an efficient s, unless the attacker controls more than 2/3 verifiers of the whole P2P network[1].

With the above mentioned reward operations for the verifiers, we can have several payout cases. For example, we specify that $d = r_d = r_v = 100$, and there $\exists v_i$ reporting the verification result. Therefore, we can have the following reward payout cases.

Case 1. When there is no v_i in the minority group, i.e., $n_{minor} = 0$, we specify $r_{v-min} = 0$ so that $r_{v-max} = 100$. Hence, each v in the majority group will get $r_{per-major} = \frac{100}{n_{major}}$ tokens as reward.

Case 2. When there is v_i in the minority group while $n_{minor} \neq n_{major}$, we specify $r_{v-min} = 1$ so that $r_{v-max} = 99$. Thus, each v in the majority group will get $r_{per-major} = \frac{99}{n_{major}}$ tokens as reward, and each v in the minority group will get $r_{per-minor} = \frac{1}{n_{minor}}$ tokens as reward.

Case 3. When $n_{minor} = n_{major}$, each v that reports verification result will get $r_{per-v} = \frac{100}{n_v}$ tokens equally as reward.

Algorithm (1) presents the verifier's reward payout algorithm, which includes the above three cases.

One example of the approach regarding verifying a detection signature as efficiency is illustrated by Fig. 2. In this instance, the P2P network has 5 participants. One p as a donor submits an SFID called "DS-file1" with 100 tokens as deposit to the smart contract. The other four participants play as v to verify the efficiency of the detection signature. Among these verifiers, three of them report

---

[1] By contrast, to make an efficient s become inefficient, the collusive verification only needs more than 1/3 verifiers of the whole P2P network. In our system, we consider the "inefficiency becomes efficiency" more dangerous than the other way round.

Algorithm 1. Verifier's Reward Payout Algorithm

Require: 100 tokens deposited
Ensure: $\exists v_i$ reporting verification result

1: **if** $n_{major} == n_{minor}$ **then**
2:     $r_{per-v} = \frac{100}{n_v}$
3: **else**
4:     **if** $n_{minor} == 0$ **then**
5:        $r_{per-major} = \frac{100}{n_{major}}$
6:     **else**
7:        $r_{per-major} = \frac{99}{n_{major}}$
8:        $r_{per-minor} = \frac{1}{n_{minor}}$
9:     **end if**
10: **end if**

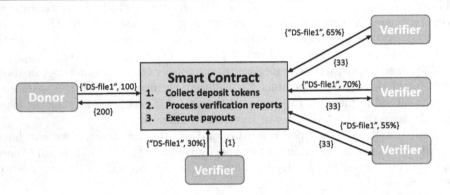

Fig. 2. Sample interactions between the participants in our approach when a detection signature is judged as efficiency.

the efficiency of DS-file1 greater than 50% (i.e., 65%, 70% and 55% respectively), while one of them reports that this detection signature is inefficient since the efficiency is only 30%. Upon that, the smart contract makes the consensus decision in terms of the majority results and judges DS-file1 as an efficient detection signature. Thereafter, the smart contract returns the deposit 100 tokens and an extra reward with another 100 tokens, i.e., 200 tokens altogether, to the donor as it contributes an efficient detection signature to the whole system. Also, the smart contract rewards the verifiers who report the verification results according to the reward payout algorithm (see Algorithm (1)). Therefore, the smart contract splits the 99 tokens proportionally in terms of the number of the majority verifiers, i.e., 33 tokens per majority verifier, while still gives 1 token to the minority verifier who claims that the detection signature is inefficient.

Because the design principal of the retribution mechanism is to encourage every participant to work for verification, even though the result makes a verifier belong to the minority group, the verifier still gets a minimized reward, but surely the result making the verifier belong to the majority group will lead to a maximized profit for the verifier.

5   Implementation

This section presents the prototype including the system implementation and the token values setup for validating the proposed approach.

For implementing the system, the participant nodes are deployed on Cloud-Lab with the virtual machine (VM) running Ubuntu 18-64-STD by default setting. On each node, we install Ethereum (Geth version 1.9.16-stable) and Solidity (version 0.5.16) for solidity files compilation. Thus, we use those nodes to generate a real premissioned blockchain P2P network. Truffle (version 5.1.34) is used to deploy the complied smart contracts on the locally created Ethereum blockchain network. We also use web3.js (version 1.2.1) and truffle-contract (version 4.0.31) to interact with the smart contract functions from our JavaScript files. Also, we employ IPFS to physically store the real detection signature files while only spread SFID on the blockchain.

The voting smart contract mainly consists of three functions, i.e., push SFID, consensus, and reward payout. The push SFID function is used to allow the donor to submit the detection signature to the blockchain P2P network, the consensus function aims to tally up the verification results sent by the verifiers, and the reward payout function is implemented in compliance with the retribution mechanism.

Furthermore, regarding the token values setup in a permissioned blockchain, the smart contract is initialized with a high amount of tokens to ensure that the system has enough funds for rewarding the participants who make contribution and in turn ensuring that the system can keep functioning for a long term. For instance, the smart contract is initialized with 10 million tokens, and each participant in the P2P network is credited with 1000 tokens initially by the smart contract. The donor node has to firstly deposit 100 tokens with the smart contract before it can write a SFID to the smart contract. Also, we specify the extra reward for the donor as 100 tokens and the total reward for the verifiers as 100 tokens as well.

In addition, the number of participant nodes (including donor and verifier) could vary from 10 to 100 in our experiment setting. More details are presented in the following experimental results.

6   Experiments

The section shows that several experiments are conducted built on the prototype implementation, and the corresponding experimental results are presented for evaluating our approach.

6.1   Computation Performance

First of all, we test the computation performance for carrying out different tasks based on the prototype. Table 2 shows the computation overhead including CPU usage, memory usage and execution time in terms of the corresponding tasks.

Table 2. Performance of different tasks on blockchain.

Task	CPU (%)	MEM (MB)	Exec. Time (ms)
Run geth	1.22	305.814	–
Deploy smart contracts	3.12	685.013	1683
Push SFID	4.72	68.36	144.63
Consensus	5.31	75.89	208.77
Reward payout	4.94	62.52	178.04

The blockchain network is initiated by running the Ethereum client (Geth) and connecting the nodes with each other for forming the P2P network. This Geth process continues running and takes 1.22% of the CPU and 305.814 MB of the memory. Once the Ethereum nodes are initialized and connected with each other, the smart contracts are then deployed to the blockchain network. This process takes 3.12% of the CPU and 685.013 MB of the memory as it covers many steps like the compilation of the smart contracts, initialization of smart contracts, and finally deployment to the blockchain network. This process lasts 1683 ms (around 1.6 s).

The push SFID task utilizes around 4.72% of the CPU, takes 68.36 MB of the memory, and spends around 144.64 ms for execution. Comparably, the reward payout task utilizes around 4.94% of the CPU, takes 62.52 MB of the memory, and spends around 178.04 ms for execution. The consensus task takes CPU utilization of 5.31%, which is greater than the push SFID task and the reward payout task, as the consensus task has higher complexity involved, i.e., it has to keep track of the verification results sent by all the verifiers and maintain the track of the participants belonging to the majority group and the minority group respectively. The memory usage of the consensus task is also higher than the push SFID task and the reward payout task, since the consensus task involves maintaining the variables and array for storing the incoming efficiency results from the verifiers, and also, it stores the information about the participant IDs of the majority group and the minority group. Consequently, the consensus task spends more time around 208.77 ms for execution.

6.2 Reward per Majority Verifier

We emulate the reward tokens for each majority verifier when there is no minority verifiers and the submitted detection signature is verified as efficient. Figure 3 shows the result. It is apparent that the more majority verifiers involved, the less reward each majority verifier can obtain. We can see that when the majority group includes only 10 verifiers, each one can gain 10 tokens as reward, however, when the majority group includes 100 verifiers, each one can only gain 1 token as reward. That result informs that the deposit should be reconciled with the scale of the P2P network, less deposit will decrease the verifiers' incentive to perform verification.

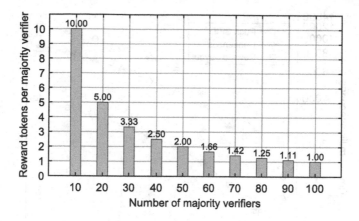

Fig. 3. Reward per majority verifier.

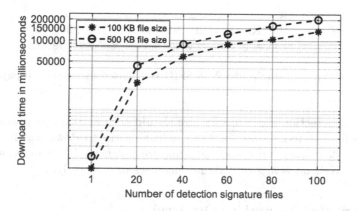

Fig. 4. Detection file download time cost.

6.3 Detection File Download Time Cost

Figure 4 shows the time cost for downloading the detection files from IPFS. We measure two sorts of files, i.e., one sort that the file size is 100 KB, and the other sort that the file size is 500 KB. Note that in our system, each file just contains one detection signature, and so the file sizes selected here are just in terms of the typical cases in practice. When the verifier only needs to download one detection signature file, it takes 1,445 ms for the 100 KB file size and 2,139 ms for the 500 KB file size on average respectively. It is obvious that the bigger file costs more time for downloading. For example, when 100 verifiers go to download one hundred 500 KB files, it takes 201,869 ms ($\sim$202 s) altogether, by contrast, when they go to download one hundred 100 KB files, it only takes 136,909 ms ($\sim$137 s) altogether. Further, according to the figure, we can see that the file-download time for the 500 KB file size increases much faster than the 100 KB file size, as the slope of the curve with the 500 KB file size is much steeper.

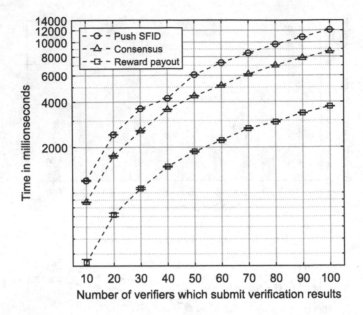

Fig. 5. Networking overheads: Push SFID vs. Consensus vs Reward payout.

Thus, the detection signature file size should keep as small as possible, otherwise it will cost more time for the whole verifiers to download it. Though the verifiers download the detection signature file from IPFS in parallel, the networking overhead is aggregated and increases dramatically.

6.4   Distributed Networking Overhead

Figure 5 presents the networking overheads in terms of the increasing number of verifiers. It includes three curves, i.e., the push SFID time cost, the consensus time cost and the reward payout time cost using average values with 95% confidence interval. We can see that when there are 10 verifiers, it spends 1202.63 ms for carrying out the push SFID task, 868.318 ms for performing the consensus task, and 351.052 ms for taking the reward payout task. Also, when there are 100 verifiers on the P2P network, it spends 1208.6 vs. 8672.6 ms vs. 3726.28 ms, respectively.

The push SFID task takes the largest networking overhead. This is because during the push SFID process, the smart contract first checks whether the donor node has enough tokens for deposit or not. After checking, it stores the SFID value in temporary storage and emits an event notifying all the other participants in the network that a new SFID has been pushed to the smart contract. This further triggers the consensus process.

The networking overhead of the consensus task is greater than the reward payout task, as the smart contract has to keep track of the efficiency percentage result sent by each participant. Also, in the consensus process, the smart contract keeps track of the number of participants in both the majority group and the minority group.

In addition, the reward payout task takes the least networking overhead, since it utilizes the computation result calculated by the consensus function about the participant IDs which come under either the majority group or the minority group. The reward payout function then uses this information stored by the consensus process to distribute the tokens among the majority group and the minority group accordingly.

7 Conclusion

Collaborative intrusion detection system (CIDS) has a global view against the network attack, whereby the shared security information including the detection signature can help to build a coordinated defense. However, the existing CIDSes often neglect the efficiency of the shared security information, which actually not only consumes the storage resource and wastes the computational process, but also brings security problems as the inefficient detection signature will raise the false alert ratio. In this paper, we proposed a blockchain-based retribution mechanism to incentivize the participants to verify the efficiency of the shared detection signature for the CIDS. Thanks to the Ethereum blockchain financial nature and the smart contract programmability, we facilitated the incentivization by using Ethereum tokens and the distributed consensus with the smart contract pBFT-based voting. The prototype and the corresponding experiments demonstrated the effectiveness of the proposed approach.

Acknowledgment. This work was supported in part by XJTLU Research Development Funding RDF-21-02-012 and XJTLU Teaching Development Funding TDF21/22-R24-177.

References

1. Anderson, H.: Introduction to NESSUS. Retrieved from Symantec (2003)
2. Benet, J.: IPFS-content addressed, versioned, P2P file system (DRAFT 3). arXiv preprint arXiv:1407.3561 (2014)
3. Bolzoni, D., Crispo, B., Etalle, S.: ATLANTIDES: an architecture for alert verification in network intrusion detection systems. In: LISA, vol. 7, pp. 1–12 (2007)
4. Chaboya, D.J., Raines, R.A., Baldwin, R.O., Mullins, B.E.: Network intrusion detection: automated and manual methods prone to attack and evasion. IEEE Secur. Priv. **4**(6), 36–43 (2006)
5. Chadwick, D.W., et al.: A cloud-edge based data security architecture for sharing and analysing cyber threat information. Futur. Gener. Comput. Syst. **102**, 710–722 (2020)

6. Fan, W., Park, Y., Kumar, S., Ganta, P., Zhou, X., Chang, S.Y.: Blockchain-enabled collaborative intrusion detection in software defined networks. In: 2020 IEEE 19th International Conference on Trust, Security and Privacy in Computing and Communications (TrustCom), pp. 967–974 (2020)
7. Fan, W., et al.: Enabling privacy-preserving sharing of cyber threat information in the cloud. In: 2019 6th IEEE International Conference on Cyber Security and Cloud Computing (CSCloud)/ 2019 5th IEEE International Conference on Edge Computing and Scalable Cloud (EdgeCom), pp. 74–80 (2019)
8. Gai, F., Wang, B., Deng, W., Peng, W.: Proof of reputation: a reputation-based consensus protocol for peer-to-peer network. In: Pei, J., Manolopoulos, Y., Sadiq, S., Li, J. (eds.) DASFAA 2018. LNCS, vol. 10828, pp. 666–681. Springer, Cham (2018). https://doi.org/10.1007/978-3-319-91458-9_41
9. Gilad, Y., Hemo, R., Micali, S., Vlachos, G., Zeldovich, N.: Algorand: scaling byzantine agreements for cryptocurrencies. In: Proceedings of the 26th Symposium on Operating Systems Principles, pp. 51–68 (2017)
10. Zhou, J., Carlson, A.J., Bishop, M.: Verify results of network intrusion alerts using lightweight protocol analysis. In: 21st Annual Computer Security Applications Conference (ACSAC 2005), pp. 10–126 (2005)
11. Li, W., Wang, Yu., Li, J., Au, M.H.: Towards blockchained challenge-based collaborative intrusion detection. In: Zhou, J., et al. (eds.) ACNS 2019. LNCS, vol. 11605, pp. 122–139. Springer, Cham (2019). https://doi.org/10.1007/978-3-030-29729-9_7
12. Matsumoto, S., Reischuk, R.M.: IKP: turning a PKI around with decentralized automated incentives. In: 2017 IEEE Symposium on Security and Privacy (SP), pp. 410–426 (2017)
13. Putra, G.D., Dedeoglu, V., Pathak, A., Kanhere, S.S., Jurdak, R.: Decentralised trustworthy collaborative intrusion detection system for IoT. In: 2021 IEEE International Conference on Blockchain (Blockchain), pp. 306–313 (2021)
14. Qin, D., Wang, C., Jiang, Y.: RPchain: a blockchain-based academic social networking service for credible reputation building. In: Chen, S., Wang, H., Zhang, L.-J. (eds.) ICBC 2018. LNCS, vol. 10974, pp. 183–198. Springer, Cham (2018). https://doi.org/10.1007/978-3-319-94478-4_13
15. Subba, B., Biswas, S., Karmakar, S.: False alarm reduction in signature-based IDS: game theory approach. Secur. Commun. Netw. 9(18), 4863–4881 (2016)
16. Tug, S., Meng, W., Wang, Y.: CBSigIDS: towards collaborative blockchained signature-based intrusion detection. In: 2018 IEEE International Conference on Internet of Things (iThings) and IEEE Green Computing and Communications (GreenCom) and IEEE Cyber, Physical and Social Computing (CPSCom) and IEEE Smart Data (SmartData), pp. 1228–1235 (2018)
17. Vasilomanolakis, E., Karuppayah, S., Mühlhäuser, M., Fischer, M.: Taxonomy and survey of collaborative intrusion detection. ACM Comput. Surv. 47(4), 1–33 (2015)
18. Zhou, C.V., Leckie, C., Karunasekera, S.: A survey of coordinated attacks and collaborative intrusion detection. Comput. Secur. 29(1), 124–140 (2010)
19. Zhuang, Q., Liu, Y., Chen, L., Ai, Z.: Proof of reputation: a reputation-based consensus protocol for blockchain based systems. In: Proceedings of the 2019 International Electronics Communication Conference, pp. 131–138 (2019)

Smart Contracts in the Cloud

Luis Angel D. Bathen[✉] and Divyesh Jadav

IBM Research, New York, USA
{bathen,divyesh}@us.ibm.com

Abstract. The emergence of crypto currencies such as Bitcoin and Ethereum have shown the value in decentralized technologies. The idea of having 24/7 access to programmable money peaked the interest in the field, and as a by-product, came the realization that the same core technologies that enable programmable dog money, can enable highly-available DNS services, highly-available storage services, 24/7 asset exchanges, and peer-to-peer marketplaces to name a few. This paper explores the use of smart contracts in multi-cloud environments in order to facilitate business processes across multiple providers speaking different languages in terms of policies, best practices, APIs, and SLAs.

Keywords: Blockchain · Decentralied applications · Smart contracts · Cloud

1 Introduction

Never before has a digital cash system been able to capture the attention of major retailers, the media, and governments as Bitcoin [30], Ethereum [18], and the many other alt-coin variants. Crypto-currencies became very appealing with their promise of programmable money [9]. However, their true value is in their enabling technologies, the *blockchain* and *smart-contracts*. These technologies made it possible to design systems that could transact given a set of business logic. In 2021, Blockchain funding grew 713% YoY to reach 25.5Bn USD [8]. Such rapid influx of funding has led to the emergence of new concepts such as Decentralized Finance (DeFi) [33] and Web3.0 [39].

DeFi alone has well over 113Bn USD in funds locked by smart-contracts [33], this means, programmable money locked by different applications running on various blockchain platforms. This includes items such as Non-Fungible Tokens [14], crypto-exchanges, crypto-lending, etc. Web 3.0 on the other hand intends to remove the middle man from most interactions, making most applications true peer-to-peer and fully decentralized.

Meanwhile, the Bitcoin network has shown to be highly resilient, provides high availability and trust in its immutable ledger thanks to its proof-of-work consensus mechanism [16,17]. The Ethereum network [18] does not fall behind and provides more complex smart contracts. Blockchain at its core leverages several concepts in the crypto community, from one-way hash chains [23,34], to forward security [6], signature aggregation [29], as well as concepts from game theory [28].

© The Author(s) 2022
L. Bathen et al. (Eds.): SVCC 2022, CCIS 1683, pp. 74–89, 2022.
https://doi.org/10.1007/978-3-031-24049-2_5

Though they have their limitations, Bitcoin and Ethereum proved the viability of decentralization at scale and their success motivated the next generation of blockchain technologies [2,10,12,19].

Besides high availability, immutability, and the ability to run business logic, decentralized applications benefit from the transparency of the logic running within their blockchain networks. This means that we can verify what code is running, and what data is being fed to the business logic. This makes it ideal for scenarios where parties need to collaborate and guarantee that the intended logic runs. Moreover, in the event something happens, blockchains are fully auditable and code execution can be replayed. This enables us to design systems that leverage blockchain technology to manage systems where multiple parties need to participate without having to fully trust eachother.

This paper explores the use of blockchain in the context of multi-cloud/hybrid-could environments. We present a storage tiering system that relies on smart contracts to manage volume tiering and migration policies across various cloud providers.

2   Background

2.1   Bitcoin Blockchain

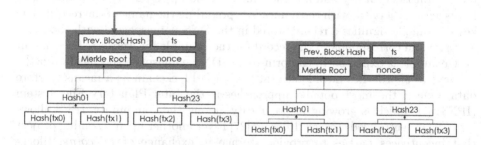

Fig. 1. Blockchain diagram

Bitcoin is structured as a peer-to-peer (P2P) network architecture on top of the Internet. Each full node in the blockchain contains a full copy of the entire blockchain, which contains all transactions dating back to the original *Genesis* block (Fig. 1). This allows blocks to validate new blocks/transactions, while at the same time, provide a high-degree of redundancy. Each full node requires several tens of GBs of storage in order to maintain a full copy of the block chain. Blocks are added to the network via consensus, which can be as energy-hungry as Bitcoin's proof-of-work, to more traditional approaches such as Hyperledger Fabric's Kafka-based ordering service [1,12].

2.2 Decentralized Applications

Decentralized applications (*dApps*) were first introduced by Bitcoin [30]. Applications such as Namecoin or Colored coins used the ledger as a secure data store, where they used the *OP_RETURN* operator/instruction to store encoded data that could be publically verifiable. Ethereum further improved on the idea of smart contracts by introducing the Ethereum Virtual Machine (EVM) and its own programming language called Solidity [18]. The EVM allowed for more complex programming models and implementations, thus becoming the de-factor ledger of choice for most *dApps*. HLF [1,12] introduced the concept of *chaincode* (smart-contracts) running within their own containers, which enables environment reproducibility. Unline the EVM, which requires code written in Solidity, HLF supports golang natively, and has added support for other languages such as Java and NodeJS.

Namecoin [32] was one of the first projects to leverage the Bitcoin blockchain to build a decentralized version of a critical legacy system (DNS). Namecoin's DNS service was built around the Bitcoin blockchain, where entries were to be stored as metadata within the blockchain using the *OP_RETURN* operator. Due to the limitations of the Bitcoin blockchain, Namecoin decided to do a full fork plus some additions of the Bitcoin code base. The blockchain allows DNS entries to be registered within the Namecoin blockchain, making domain ownership immutable and agreed upon a large number of parties. Each Namecoin record consists of a key and a value which can be up to 520 bytes in size. Each key is actually a path, with the namespace preceding the name of the record. The key d/example signifies a record stored in the DNS namespace d with the name example and corresponds to the record for the example.bit website. The content of d/example is expected to conform to the DNS namespace specification [31].

Several approaches have looked at using the blockchain as a means to store data. One of the most popular approaches is the Inter-Planetary File System (IPFS) [7], which is growing in popularity among the community. IPFS allows for truly decentralized storage. Filecoin [27] is yet another up and coming project that incentivices parties to provide storage in exchange of *filecoins*. Blockstore [36], keeps block metadata in the Bitcoin blockchain, while storing the actual block data in a *Kademlia*-like DHT (see Fig. 2). Similarly, Storj [38] and MetaDisk [37] follow a similar concept, where block metadata is stored in a traditional blockchain with a modified proof-of-work, while the data is erasure coded and distributed among storage nodes in their network.

Decentralized identity [4,5,15,22,24,25] is yet another hot topic in the Blockchain world, as it relies on granting users unrestricted access to the network. For a more comprehensive survey on decentralized applications please see [3].

Most decentralized applications rely on a front-end application (UI/UX) that allows users to interact with the blockchain. These UI/UX systems either talk to some RESTFul APIs in the form of gateways, that serve as entry points to ledgers, or they rely on a wallet type client that directly interacts with their respective blockchains via some discoverable peers. Figure 3 shows an example of a typical *dApp*, where the user is shown accessing the same blockchain via a

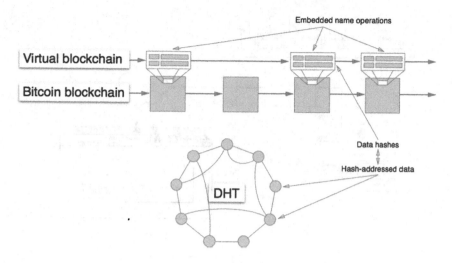

Fig. 2. Blockstore architecture

light-weight client (also known as a wallet), and through a web interface. One key difference between the two approaches is that the wallet may have access to the user's keys, which control which assets he/she owns. In this model, assets are user owned/user controlled. The second approach does key management on behalf of the user, thus, not really user controlled nor user owned as the keys that own the assets belong to the party providing the web portal. This is very common in Cryptocurrency Exchanges.

2.3   Permissioned Ledgers

Bitcoin, Ethereum, and most crypto-currency variants are known as public permissionless blockchains. Public permissionless blockchains are meant to be used by anyone who wishes it; the only requirement for participating on the network is having a client that adheres to the blockchain's protocol, and is able to discover peers associated with the ledger. Users in these networks interact via the use of public/private keys. Ideally, in such scenario, users will own the devices they use to interact with the blockchain, as well as the device that has access to the keys. As all assets owned on these blockchains are managed by their respective keys. Thus, when a *Alice* needs to send *Bob* a bitcoin, all that she needs is *Bob's* Bitcoin address, which is derived from its public key. Her wallet then constructs the transaction saying *Alice* sends $coin_i$ to *Bob*, signs it, and broadcasts it over the network. Bitcoin nodes then process the transaction by verifying that the *owner* of the $coin_i$ is indeed *Alice* by verifying against the public key provided by *Alice*.

Bitcoin's smart contract engine is stack based, so there is very limited what it can do, in this case, a simple payment verification script is computed and validated. Ethereum further enhanced its smart contract engine and made it

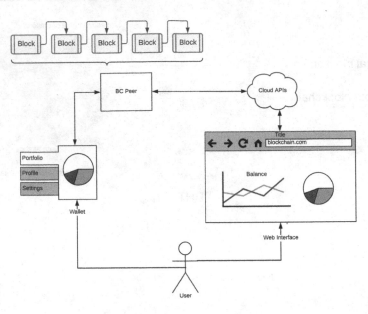

Fig. 3. dApp sample architecture

Turing-complete, thus, Ethereum became the blockchain of choice for most parties looking to deploy smart contract based applications. In this scenario, a smart contract is compiled, and its bytecode is deployed. Users then invoke the smart contract with the necessary data to execute the contract, while providing a small fee called gas. Peers then pickup the invocation request, execute it, and agree on the result via consensus. If something goes wrong, consensus will fail, however, in the event of failure, users are still charged the corresponding gas amount. Bitcoin miners charge a small fee to process the transaction, Ethereum does the same via its gas concept. This is necessary as all transactions submitted to the network must be processed, which takes up resources. Requiring transaction fees is a mechanism that incentivices nodes to provide validation/transaction processing services, as well as deterrents against possible denial of service attacks. You can further limit resources spent on a smart contract by requiring higher gas fees.

The freedom in public permissionless blockchains comes at the cost of higher transactional fees, longer transaction validation times, lower transactions processed per second, etc. The latter is due to the fact that these blockchains have to perform resource-intensive consensus protocols, that may rely on brute-force hashing. There are ledgers that try to minimize this as they move towards other types of consensus mechanisms (e.g., proof-of-stake [10,11]). Other types of blockchains include private permissionless (e.g., LTO Network), public permissioned (e.g., Sovring [20] and Ripple [13]) and private permissioned blockchains (e.g., Hyperledger Fabric [12,19]).

We choose to work with permissioned blockchains at the enterprise-level as they give us most blockchain features without the horrors of the wild-west that are present in Bitcoin or Ethereum, moreover, since permissioned blockchains require nodes to be authenticated, there is a certain amount of trust on the participants, thus, the consensus mechanism can be easier on the wallet. Moreover, since consensus can be lighter, this means that transaction throughput may be higher in permissioned blockchains.

Hyperledger Fabric (HLF) supports a plug-in based architecture for various components, including consensus. The default scheme uses Apache Kafka as its ordering service, which simple orders transactions on a per-channel basis. The idea of having separate channels allows for higher transactional throughput, as peers can process transactions for multiple channels natively.

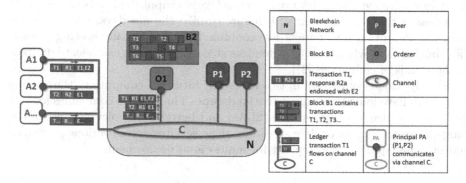

Fig. 4. Ordering service in hyperledger fabric [12]

Furthermore, HLF for example relies on the idea that a chaincode/smart contract can be packaged, and deployed on the ledger. When the chaincode is deployed and initialized, a container instance is created on each peer participating (subscribed) to the given channel (topic). This means that HLF is not a single blockchain, but rather, composed of multiple individual chains (called channels). Another benefit of the channel architecture is the data segregation, so only peers who join the same channel can see the same data. A high-level diagram of HLF's ordering service is shown in Fig. 4.

2.4 Cloud Computing

With a projected revenue of US$397.90Bn in 2022 [35], worldwide adoption of Public Cloud continues to increase YoY with an expected CAGR 2022–2027 of 15.97%. Cloud computing allows companies to reduce their overhead as they can purchase compute and storage resources on the fly based on their demans. This means that many companies may save money by adopting public offerings over hosting their own services in their own data centers, where companies need to pay for servers, IT departments, electricity, cooling, premises, etc. Rather, for some companies it is more cost effective to run lean IT departments and rely heavily on the cloud. In some scenarios such move to the cloud may not be cost effective or feasible. For example, companies with strict data compliance policies may not be allowed to export data outside of their premises/geo locations. Another reason is that some companies may prefer to optimize their own IT environments in order to achieve better cost. This is why sometimes cloud-heavy companies choose to move back from the cloud and run their own IT infrastructures. Some companies may choose to take a hybrid approach, where they host some critical/sensitive services on premise, while hosting other public cloud friendly services in the cloud.

Though cloud computing has many pros, they are multi-tenant in nature, thus, when a company uses cloud resources, they are actually sharing said resources with other companies. In a sense, as cloud providers grow, they continue to centralize (from a service perspective) compute and storage services. This means that in the event of a failure, unlike the old days, when a server fails, the disruption was more or less contained to the company hosting the service. In this case, when there is a cloud service disruption, it can affect hundreds or thousands of companies [21].

Finally, cloud computing in general is the future of computing, thus, many companies have joined its competitive landscape. This enables companies looking for better service level agreements (SLAs) and better fault-tolerance, as well as competitive pricing, to explore spreading their services across various providers, and in many applications, support for multi-cloud deployments.

3 Smart-Contracts in the Cloud

One of the benefits of having competition in the cloud space besides pressured innovation and better pricing, is the ability to spread application deployments across various clouds, be it multiple public clouds, or hybrid-cloud environments. This means that applications have to talk different languages (e.g., different cloud APIs) as well as different SLAs. Such ecosystem is composed of multiple parties that need to trust in a programmable way, where business logics can map to policies and SLAs. These types of deployments are low-hanging fruit opportunities for Blockchain. Blockchain, would privide a trusted common platform for multi-cloud applications to deploy business logic that is agreeable across various parties. It is transparent, auditable, and highly available. All qualities of outmost importance in today's rapid evolving IT world.

This section will explore one such use case that leverages the concept of multi-cloud in conuction with blockchain technology in order to provide a common platform for the management and deployment of common IT service technologies such as Information Life Cycle Management, Storage Tiering, Change Management, etc.

3.1 Storage Tiering

Overview. Storage tiering helps organizations strike a balance between performance and cost by moving data around different tiers to cope with swings in demand. Tiering ensures that data sits on the most appropriate storage fabric according to the application's needs, be it latency or throughput. Most research efforts have focused on traditional storage systems and tiering across different disk types. For instance, hot data residing in Tier 2 (high endurance, high capacity, 10K RPM HDs) can be migrated to high performance, high cost SSDs. This process is called up-tiering, where you go from a lower class tier to a higher class tier. Similarly, you can migrate cold data from a high tier (T1) to a colder tier (T2). There are many types of tiers. There are usually several rules of thumb with respect to how to map data to the right tier. For this, one of the main metrics dynamic tiering systems use is IO density, which is a function of IO/second/GB. Based on IO density we might decide to up-tier or down-tier storage. Tiering can be done for object storage, file storage, and of course, the most popular, block storage. For Object/File storage you would look primarily at access rate, whereas block storage you look primarily at IO density.

Table 1. Tier/IO density mapping for block storage

Storage Volume Tier Level	IO Density (IO/second/GB)
Tier0	>=1
Tier1a	0.7 - 1.0
Tier1b	0.5 - 0.7
Tier2	0.1 - 0.5
Tier3	0.01 - 0.1
Nearline	0.0 - 0.01
Inactie	0
Unknown	Null

Table 1 shows a traditional rule-of-thumb mapping between a tier and its applicable IO Density. System administrators/automated systems will use these metrics to decide where a particular volume should be mapped. Up/Down-tiering a volume involves copying and moving a volume across tiers, these tiers could be within a data center (traditionally), across data centers (same organization/-cloud), and across different organizations (e.g., a hybrid-cloud model). Tiering has many great benefits, but if not done right (e.g., not using the right policy), there are many things that could go wrong, from a simple mistake like putting a volume on the wrong tier, to more serious problems where the volume is lost in-transit with no one to hold accountable. For instance, if a volume is pushed to a tier in a remote organization (e.g., third party cloud), and the volume never makes it to the remote organization, the question is then, what happened? Who is accountable? The third party that provides the block storage service? The system administrator that defined the tiering policy? The engine that executed the policy and did not check that the volume had made it to the third party cloud (new tier)? What if an error in a policy resulted in massive losses for a client, and in order to avoid consequences, the responsible party tampers with the policy? Can they then deny any wrongdoing?

Our approach tries to solve these issues by providing a way to execute policies in an automated fashion, while at the same time providing the means to have accountability for such scenarios. We build on the concept of smart contracts, where we have a fabric that will execute a policy (a smart contract), that has been agreed upon and signed by multiple parties (the system administrator, management, the third party storage provider, etc.), with the goal of introducing accountability into the tiering process.

Storage Volume Tiering. Figure 5 shows a high level diagram of a traditional tiering solution. Storage is allocated and pooled into different tiers, in this example, three tiers, Gold, Silver, and Bronze. When a file system is created/-mounted, you then request to place the file system on a particular tier based on business needs, performance needs, etc. This process follows simple rules developed by system administrators. Similar to the block storage scenario, what tier to choose is left to the system administrator, or an automated system guided by a set of policies/rules designed by the system administrator. Automated tiering solutions like IBM's Easy Tier, EMC's Fully Automated Storage Tiering, and HP/3PAR's Adaptive Optimization, all rely on policies and best practices for tiering. These polices are executed by a centralized server/manager, and pre-defined. Often pre-agreed on, however, when you start engaging other parties, the question then becomes, what policy should be implemented given that in a multi-service provider environment, different best practices may be followed, thus ending in scenarios where the end result deviates from what each party involved in the tiering transaction expected. For instance, consider a scenario where we follow Provider A's guidelines for tiering based on best practices defined by our architects, but once we start using tiers provided by third parties, which may have their own policies for tiering, if our expectations are that IO density of 0.1–0.5 (exclusive) should go to Tier2, but the third party storage provider says 0.1–0.5 (inclusive) is Tier1. We want to down-tier, they want to up-tear, thus leading to problems with respect to where data should reside. If something were to happen where we cause downtime due to a tiering issue, the question then arises, who is at fault? Both parties are following their own guidelines and best practices. For example, our policy says Inactive and unmapped volumes (not associated with a host - orphan) can be reclaimed, but a third party says such volumes are just inactive, thus must be kept in Tier3. Or vice versa. Let's say a volume is deleted/reclaimed, who is to blame? What policy was followed? This is particularly important when dealing with information life cycle management (ILM) as a whole as it can be applied to tiering as well as backup and retention policies.

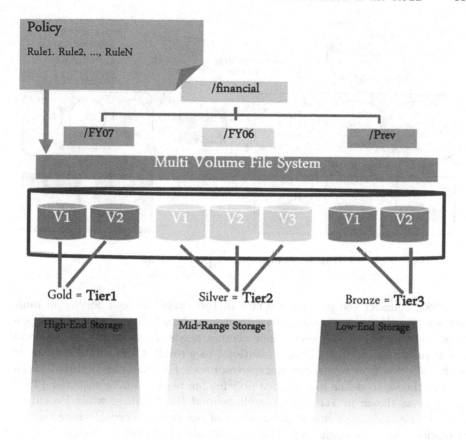

Fig. 5. Traditional tiering solution [26]

Leveraging Smart Contracts. In this work we propose the use of smart-contracts to solve the best practices, policy mismatch, and provenance problem inherent in today's storage tiering and ILM solutions. Our work can be extended to object, file, and block storage as our engine is technology agnostic. Similarly, we could extend this work to incorporate other aspects of ILM such as backup, recovery, and retention policies. Figure 6 shows a high-level diagram of our approach. The blockchain fabric will be used to serve two purposes: 1) Provide provenance of tiering/ILM actions by recording events in the form of provenance metadata (e.g., hashes of what data is tiered, how much data, time, etc.), this data is immutable, so there is no way to tamper with it. 2) We will use HLF [1] for executing policies in the form of chaincode. In our multi-cloud environment we assume each cloud provider is represented as an organization, and each organization can have any number of peers. Our chaincode endorsement policies require at least one peer per organization to agree for consensus. We use leveldb for a richer world state in order to support dynamic tiering look-up tables.

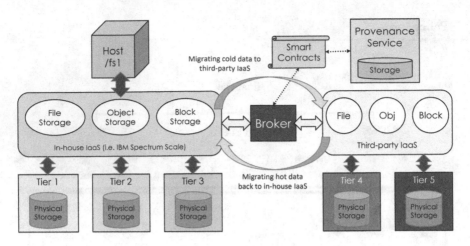

Fig. 6. Smart-contract based tiering

First, consider the problem we face in Infrastructure-as-a-Service in multi-Service provider environments, where storage architects have designed best practices and policies to best serve their client's needs. As stated before, different teams may come up with different solutions, as a result, there will be a mismatch with respect to how to manage storage resources. For example, tiering, Provider A may choose to define fine grained policies for tiering, where each tier (Tier0-Niactive as shown in Table 1) has well defined IO densities, while Provider B may choose to define a coarser grained set of policies for tiering, where each tier is mapped to a premium level (a more abstract Gold, Silver, Bronze model as shown in Fig. 5). In this scenario, the question then comes, a volume with 0.5 IO density is mapped to Tier1b, Tier2, or Gold or Silver? This mapping needs to be agreed on, and represented in an abstract model so that we can represented in a generic, simple, yet auditable and error-proof contract that can be executed. And in the event of an error with respect to where a volume is mapped, the contract can be audited and there is non-repudiation as the storage architects/administrators involved in the transaction signed off on the contract. Once a mapping is agreed upon, the next step is to define the logic that will simply tiering across organization boundaries. For instance, take Fig. 7, when a volume enters provider B's boundaries, the logic within Fig. 7 applies. If the volume's IO density is high, the volume will reside within *GOLD TIER*. Provider A would have agreed to set the threshold of > 0.5 as *GOLD TIER*, so that in the event that a volume goes through up-tiering/down-tiering, we will be able to assign it to the right tier. Similarly, if a volume crosses Provider A's boundary, there should be a clear distinction in IO load between GOLD, BRONZE, and SILVER. This is because each provider charges different premiums for the different tiers. For instance, Tier0-Tier2 in Provider A is equivalent the Gold tier in Provider B, with respect to IO load but pricing is much different. For instance, Provider A's premium fee for Tier0 is much higher than Tier1, while Provider B's premium for the Gold tier is equivalent to Tier1b/Tier2. As a result, in the event volumes going from Provider B to Provider A, Provider B might want to state that for his/her Gold tier volumes, they should be mapped to Tier1b/Tier2 in order to respect the SLA guarantees offered to the consumer without incurring extra cost due to tiering. Now, smart contracts can go beyond simple thresholds and incorporate things like aggressive/conservative policies (last 45 historical, spike, up/down tier) and the window-throttle for tiering (sync-rate).

```
def execute_policy(volume, policy, party_signatures):

    if volume.io_density >= policy.high_io_density:

        volume.tier = GOLD_TIER

    elif volume.io_density > policy.medium_io_density and
            volume.io_density < policy.high_io_density:

        volume.tier = SILVER_TIER

    else:

        volume.tier = BRONZE_TIER

    # if parties signed the policy
    if valid_signatures(policy, party_signatures):

        execute_tiering_logic(volume, policy)
```

Fig. 7. Tiering chaincode pseudocode

Once the policy has been abstracted, it is represented in chaincode as shown in Fig. 7. All parties involved in managing the storage backend (e.g., our data center admin, the third-party storage provider) will review and agree on the chaincode to be executed. This chainode will exist within a common repository where we have version tracking, users can push code/comments, and do audits. The idea is that there will be full transparency in the process. Now, once the chaincode is agreed upon, all parties (e.g., Party A and Party B) sign the code, and the code is deployed within the blockchain fabric. The idea is that once code is agreed upon, parties cannot deny reviewing it in case something goes wrong. This will give us non-repudiation, so parties are forced to review and sign on any commonly agreed policy. Because without the signatures (acknowledgement from parties), the policy will not execute. Moreover, since this goes into an automated system, whenever a volume's IO exceeds a tier's threshold, the data/volume is then submitted to the blockchain fabric, where the chaincode to evaluate the volume information is invoked, and the policy is executed by the fabric. Once tiering is done, in the event somethings goes wrong, auditors can go back in time and see when tiering was triggered, and what policy was executed (e.g., what chaincode was invoked). This also points to the repository that contains the policy, all of it being immutable so no single party can tamper with the policy or deny on agreeing on a particular policy.

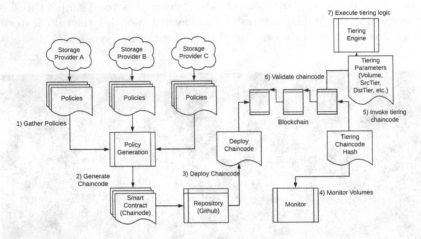

Fig. 8. SmartContract-based tiering and information life cycle management for storage infrastructure-as-a-service in a multi-service provider environment

Architecture. Figure 8 shows the steps involved in generating and executed smart contracts for the tiering/ILM context:

1. All parties define their tiering policies
2. The policy generation engine consolidates those policies and represents them as a smart contract
3. The smart contract goes through a review process following a devops process and gets deployed on the blockchain fabric
4. The monitoring engine tracks Volume IO (File IO, Object Reads/Writes, etc.), and periodically invokes the policy chaincode based on a tunable window. Furthermore, the monitor is responsible for validating the state of the system, and check if it does indeed reflect the state in the blockchain. When volumes are down/up-tiered, the world state of the system changes within the blockchain fabric itself. So outside parties cannot modify the state of the system without the monitor finding out.
5. The monitoring engine invokes the policy chaincode via its hash
6. The chaincode validates signatures and executes in the different peer-nodes, running consensus on wether to tier, not tier (backup or not, migrate or not, etc.)
7. Finally, the chaincode invokes the tiering engine to execute the up/down-tier operation for the particular volume (or file/object).

In the above model, the monitor and the tiering engine are oracles outside of the blockchain, however, nothing would prevent us from running monitoring chaincode that validate the state of the system. Similarly, the tiering engine logic could also run within the blockchain fabric. This would also allow us to provide a high-availability service, so even if one node goes done, the rest of the network can still operate, and tiering/ILM functionality is not lost. Although we focus on storage tiering/ILM, we can extend this process to many other storage management techniques. Each component in our infrastructure writes provenance data onto the blockchain describing the different actions each component took. Be it executing a tier policy, or how much data/number objects/number files and tier source/destinations, or which chaincode was deployed by which parties. This will allow us to have full transparency and provide auditing logic.

Each participating cloud provider could run a number of peers, thus, they could fully monitor all the events in the tiering ecosystem, to make sure that their SLAs are being respected, while performing the proper analytics and event monitoring to provide optimal SLAs.

4   Conclusion and Future Work

In this paper we discussed the use of smart contracts in an enterprise scenario. We showed a simple implementation of a storage tiering engine that allows volume tiering across multi-cloud environments with the assistance of a private permissioned fabric. Future work includes exploring the use of dynamic pricing for volume migration across cloud providers.

References

1. Androulaki, E., et al.: Hyperledger fabric: a distributed operating system for permissioned blockchains, pp. 30:1 30:15. EuroSys (2018)
2. Association, L.: Libra white paper. https://libra.org/en-US/white-paper/
3. Banoth, R., Dave, M.B.: A survey on decentralized application based on blockchain platform. In: 2022 International Conference on Sustainable Computing and Data Communication Systems (ICSCDS), pp. 1171–1174 (2022). https://doi.org/10.1109/ICSCDS53736.2022.9760861
4. Bathen, L., et al.: Selfis: Self-sovereign biometric ids. In: The IEEE Conference on Computer Vision and Pattern Recognition (CVPR) Workshops (2019)
5. Bathen, L.A.D., Flores, G.H., Jadav, D.: Riders: towards a privacy-aware decentralized self-driving ride-sharing ecosystem. In: 2020 IEEE International Conference on Decentralized Applications and Infrastructures (DAPPS), pp. 32–41 (2020)
6. Bellare, M., Yee, B.: Forward-security in private-key cryptography. In: Joye, M. (ed.) CT-RSA 2003. LNCS, vol. 2612, pp. 1–18. Springer, Heidelberg (2003). https://doi.org/10.1007/3-540-36563-X_1
7. Benet, J.: Inter planetary file system (2017). https://github.com/ipfs/ipfs
8. CBInsights: State of blockchain 2021 report (2021). https://www.cbinsights.com/research/report/blockchain-trends-2021/

9. CoinDesk: State of bitcoin q1 2015: Record investment buoys ecosystem (2015). http://www.coindesk.com/state-of-bitcoin-q1-2015-record-investment-buoys-ecosystem/
10. Community, C.: Cardano blockchain (2022). https://cardano.org/
11. Community, E.: Proof-of-stake (PoS) (2022). https://ethereum.org/en/developers/docs/consensus-mechanisms/pos/
12. Community, H.: Hyperledger fabric (2017). https://hyperledger-fabric.readthedocs.io/en/release/
13. Community, R.: Ripple blockchain (2022). https://ripple.com/
14. Conti, R., Schmidt, J.: What is an NFT? non-fungible tokens explained (2022). https://www.forbes.com/advisor/investing/cryptocurrency/nft-non-fungible-token/
15. (DIF): Decentralized identity foundation (2017). http://identity.foundation/
16. Eisenbarth, J.P., Cholez, T., Perrin, O.: A comprehensive study of the bitcoin p2p network. In: 2021 3rd Conference on Blockchain Research & Applications for Innovative Networks and Services (BRAINS), pp. 105–112 (2021). https://doi.org/10.1109/BRAINS52497.2021.9569782
17. Feld, S., Schönfeld, M., Werner, M.: Analyzing the deployment of bitcoin's p2p network under an as-level perspective, vol. 32 (2014). https://doi.org/10.1016/j.procs.2014.05.542
18. Foundation, E.: Ethereum (2017). https://www.ethereum.org/
19. Foundation, L.: The hyperledger project (2017). https://www.hyperledger.org
20. Foundation, S.: Sovrin blockchain (2022). https://sovrin.org/
21. Gawroński, W.: The complete history of AWS outages (2022). https://awsmaniac.com/aws-outages/
22. Group, C.C.: Decentralized identifiers (dids) v0.9 (2017). https://w3c-ccg.github.io/did-spec/
23. Hu, Y.-C., Jakobsson, M., Perrig, A.: Efficient constructions for one-way hash chains. In: Ioannidis, J., Keromytis, A., Yung, M. (eds.) ACNS 2005. LNCS, vol. 3531, pp. 423–441. Springer, Heidelberg (2005). https://doi.org/10.1007/11496137_29
24. HYPR: Decentralized biometric authentication (2017). https://www.hypr.com/biometric-authentication/
25. Inc., S.T.: Digital identity network (2017). https://securekey.com/
26. Kamaraju, A.: Storage tiering for file systems and NAS (2008). https://www.snia.org/sites/default/education/tutorials/2008/fall/filesys_mng/Kamaraju-Storage_Tiering_File_and_NAS.pdf
27. Labs, P.: Filecoin: a decentralized storage network (2017). https://filecoin.io/filecoin.pdf
28. Lewenberg, Y., Bachrach, Y., Sompolinsky, Y., Zohar, A., Rosenschein, J.S.: Bitcoin mining pools: a cooperative game theoretic analysis. In: Proceedings of the 2015 International Conference on Autonomous Agents and Multiagent Systems, AAMAS 2015, International Foundation for Autonomous Agents and Multiagent Systems, Richland, SC, pp. 919–927 (2015), http://dl.acm.org/citation.cfm?id=2772879.2773270
29. Ma, D.: Practical forward secure sequential aggregate signatures. In: Proceedings of the 2008 ACM Symposium on Information, Computer and Communications Security, ASIACCS 2008, ACM, New York, NY, USA, pp. 341–352 (2008). https://doi.org/10.1145/1368310.1368361, http://doi.acm.org/10.1145/1368310.1368361
30. Nakamoto, S.: Bitcoin: A peer-to-peer electronic cash system (2008). https://bitcoin.org/bitcoin.pdf

31. Namecoin: Domain name specification (2011). https://wiki.namecoin.info/index. php?title=Domain_Name_Specification
32. Namecoin: Namecoin (2011). https://namecoin.info/
33. Openware: The state of defi in 2021 (2021). https://medium.com/openware/the-state-of-defi-in-2021-cf647402099c
34. Schneier, B., Kelsey, J.: Cryptographic support for secure logs on untrusted machines. In: Proceedings of the 7th Conference on USENIX Security Symposium, SSYM 1998, USENIX Association, Berkeley, CA, USA, vol. 7, pp. 4–4 (1998). http://dl.acm.org/citation.cfm?id=1267549.1267553
35. statista: Public cloud (2022). https://www.statista.com/outlook/tmo/public-cloud/worldwide
36. Team, O.: Blockstore: A key-value store on bitcoin (2015). http://blog.onename.com/blockstore-bitcoin/
37. Wilkinson, S., Lowry, J.: Metadisk: A blockchain-based decentralized file storage application (2014). http://metadisk.org/metadisk.pdf
38. Wilkinson, S.: Storj: A peer-to-peer cloud storage network (2014). http://storj.io/storj.pdf
39. Wood, G.: Why we need web 3.0 (2018). https://gavofyork.medium.com/why-we-need-web-3-0-5da4f2bf95ab

A Blockchain-Based Tamper-Resistant Logging Framework

Thomas H. Austin[1,2(✉)] and Fabio Di Troia[1,2]

[1] San José State University, San Jose, USA
{thomas.austin,fabio.ditroia}@sjsu.edu
[2] Silicon Valley Cybersecurity Institute, San Jose, USA

Abstract. Since its introduction in Bitcoin, the blockchain has proven to be a versatile data structure. In its role as an immutable ledger, it has grown beyond its initial use in financial transactions to be used in recording a wide variety of other useful information.

In this paper, we explore the application of the blockchain outside of its traditional decentralized, financial domain. We show how, even with only a single "mining" node, a proof-of-work blockchain can be the cornerstone of a tamper resistant logging framework. By attaching a proof-of-work to blocks of logging messages, we make it increasingly difficult for an attacker to modify those logs even after totally compromising the system. Furthermore, we discuss various strategies an attacker might take to modify the logs without detection and show how effective those evasion techniques are against statistical analysis.

Keywords: Blockchain · Tamper-resistance · Logging

1 Introduction

Since its introduction, Bitcoin [23] has revolutionized the world of finance and of distributed consensus. Systems such as Paxos [18] had previously provided decentralized consensus, but these were fairly complex systems and did not guarantee availability. In contrast, Bitcoin introduces *Nakamoto consensus*, a probabilistic consensus that provides high availability. Since its introduction, other protocols have attempted to improve upon its design. Ethereum [30] introduced quasi-Turing complete smart contracts. Tezos [11] sought more graceful evolution of a blockchain protocol by letting clients vote on blockchain proposals and automatically upgrading to successful proposals, thus avoiding many problems with *hard forks*. Several protocols sought to improve on the consensus mechanism, either by modifying the proof-of-work mechanism [16,17,22] or by eliminating it totally [7,12,15,28].

The *blockchain* is central to the design of Bitcoin[1]. With this data structure, a block is chained to the previous block by a cryptographic hash. This chain of

---

[1] We note that the original Bitcoin whitepaper [23] did not coin the term "blockchain"; rather, the author refers to a "chain of blocks".

L. Bathen et al. (Eds.): SVCC 2022, CCIS 1683, pp. 90–104, 2022.
https://doi.org/10.1007/978-3-031-24049-2_6

hashes continues back to the first block in the chain, referred to as the *genesis block*. With this design, any change made to a block invalidates all subsequent blocks. Conflicting blocks might both be valid, but blockchain protocols resolve this by clear rules for prioritizing blocks; in the case of Bitcoin, the blockchain with the most hashing power used in its computation is the highest priority.

The blockchain data structure has traditionally been used in decentralized, distributed systems. In this paper, we show how the blockchain may be useful in a centralized system.

We create a logging framework that stores its logging messages as transactions in a local proof-of-work blockchain. If the system is later compromised by an attacker, the blockchain helps to prevent the attacker from modifying the logging messages without detection. An attacker could log fraudulent messages after the compromise. They could even modify recent log messages by rewriting the blockchain and expending the necessary computation to redo the search for valid proof-of-work solutions. However, the older the message, and the more deeply that message is buried in the blockchain, the more difficult it becomes for the attacker to tamper with the log without detection.

To evaluate our idea, we implemented our logging framework using the SpartanGold blockchain framework [4]. We produced a dataset of 30 sample blockchains in JSON format, and then experimented with various attacks.

Our results show that unsophisticated attacks where an attacker simply rebuilds the blockchain from a specific block are easily detected. A more subtle attacker would modify the block times so that each rebuilt block takes only slightly longer than would be typical for a block to be produced. Our results show that the attacker can only change the block creation times by a fairly slight amount to avoid detection.

The algorithm used to detect this type of tampering is a deep learning model trained on pairs of hash IDs and timestamp differences between the current and previous block (this approximates the time required to create the current block). We noticed that the model was not able to detect such an attack when the difference between the timestamps was comparable with the average time of the creation of a legitimate block. Precisely, the model became unreliable when the range of time between the current timestamp and the previous one was between 2 and 8 s.

Our defense gives the attacker a challenging dilemma. The more aggressively the attacker increments the block time, the more likely they are to be caught; however, if they are too cautious, an outside observer might notice the change before the blockchain can be rebuilt.

2   Background and Related Work

Many have observed the potential utility of storage on the blockchain and its value in providing a public, tamper-resistant data store. Indeed, storing data on the Bitcoin blockchain was frequent enough that Bitcoin added support for an OP_RETURN opcode to allow the storage to be done in a more efficient manner.

A few protocols have focused on using storage as part of their consensus. Permacoin [22] sought to reduce Bitcoin's proof-of-work requirements by requiring that miners also prove that they are storing a portion of the Library of Congress; storage here is a "public good", and is not intended to be used for storing arbitrary data. Spacemint [25] replaces the proof-of-work portion of Bitcoin with a *proof-of-space* system; this data is "junk" data, in the sense that it has no utility outside of the protocol.

Namecoin [24] is a fork of Bitcoin focused on storing arbitrary data, acting as a decentralized and distributed key-value store. Ali et al. introduce Blockstack [2] to serve as a decentralized public-key infrastructure (PKI); their initial model used Namecoin, though they later migrated to Bitcoin due to the greater security offered by the Bitcoin network's stronger hashing power.

Ethereum offers storage on its blockchain, but it is expensive. Several blockchain protocols have attempted to provide storage, including Filecoin [10], Storj [27], Siacoin [29], and 0Chain [21].

Intrusion detection has been tackled with machine learning algorithms with promising results. Since 1980, when the first intrusion detection system (IDS) was proposed [3], the field experienced several evolving steps. Analytical and statistical techniques have recently been substituted by machine learning models due to their superiority in detecting attacks. In [9], deep learning is compared with traditional intrusion analysis showing how much more effective the application of machine learning is in this field. Another example is the survey in [1], where different machine learning techniques are analyzed and compared on network intrusion detection. The survey concludes that the most widely applied and best performing algorithm is deep learning.

Network Intrusion Detection Systems (NIDS) are among the most explored fields where we find the application of IDS; however, it has been applied in a vast range of areas, such as detecting compromised land vehicles and aerial drones. In [26], the authors explore attacks to automotive Controller Area Networks (CANs) applying machine learning techniques to identify the theft of a vehicle. The work in [14] utilizes machine learning and blockchain technology to evade intrusions in the piloting system of Unmanned Aerial Vechicles (UAVs). In this case, the blockchain is used to share and upgrade several machine learning models to ensure that the most updated one is being used at all times without external compromising.

Biometric evaluation is also applied to identify intrusion. The work in [13], for example, assumes that the intruder has access to real users' gesture data and applies Convolutional Neural Networks (CNNs) to detect tampering of the data to bypass user authentication.

While many papers [6,8,19] have approached the conjunction of blockchain technology and machine learning, there seems to be a lack in the literature when we assume a complete compromising of the machines hosting the blockchain and, thus, no applications of machine learning to detect compromised blocks have yet been proposed to the best of our knowledge.

3   Logger Design and Implementation

Our logging framework writes messages to transactions on a local blockchain, helping to ensure the integrity of logging messages even should the system hosting the logs be compromised.

In this section, we briefly give an overview of the SpartanGold blockchain framework, review the code for our logging library, and finally discuss possible future extensions for the library.

3.1   SpartanGold Overview

SpartanGold [4] is a simplified blockchain written in JavaScript designed for experimentation and education; as such, it is an ideal tool for our experiments. Like Bitcoin, it uses the hashcash protocol [5] for proof-of-work consensus. However, there are some notable differences from Bitcoin:

- SpartanGold uses an account-based model, similar to Ethereum, rather than Bitcoin's unspent transaction output (UTXO) model.
- The proof-of-work target for mining a block in SpartanGold does not adjust over time.
- SpartanGold does not support smart contracts.
- Transactions in SpartanGold are stored directly in the block, rather than in a Merkle tree [20].
- A block in SpartanGold does not have a strict size limit.

Although SpartanGold does not support smart contracts, new functionality can be introduced by extending the `Miner` or `Block` classes. The homepage for SpartanGold[2] includes several sample implementations of different blockchain protocols.

The most notable limitation of SpartanGold for our purposes is that it does not use a Merkle tree. In Bitcoin, all transactions are contained in a single hash value (the Merkle root) that is hashed during the mining process. In contrast, all transactions in SpartanGold are stored in a map; the full contents of the map are directly hashed during the mining process. As a result, if there are a large number of transactions, or even a single large transaction, the size of the block might exceed the size of the hash function's input; when this happens, the mining power required to find a block is multiplied by the number of hashing rounds required to hash the block once.

In our performance experiments, we avoided this problem by leaving the blocks at a constant size. In a real implementation, we could resolve the issue by extending SpartanGold's `Block` class to store a Merkle root of transactions rather than the transactions themselves.

---

[2] https://github.com/taustin/spartan-gold/.

3.2   Logging Framework Codebase

We adapt SpartanGold to add the functionality needed for a logging framework. In our design, every log message writes a transaction to the blockchain. Every transaction therefore must include both a logging level and the log message itself. Since the time of the log message might not correspond to the time of the block, every transaction must also include a timestamp.

Figure 1 shows the Logger class. The log levels specified as constants at the top of the file (lines 8–9) are loosely based on the log levels for Apache's Log4J logging framework[3]. Convenience methods at the end of the file (lines 52–70) write log messages at the corresponding levels. One exception is the Block_TIME level; our logging framework uses this level to track the time that the miner began searching for a proof for the block. Every block should have exactly one transaction with this log level.

The constructor (lines 13–16) initializes the blockchain, including setting the proof-of-work target (powLeadingZeroes). It calls the initializeBlockchain method (lines 35–46), which creates a new miner (line 33), makes the genesis block (lines 35–42)[4], and then triggers the miner to begin mining new blocks (line 45). (The FakeNet class (lines 32 and 43) uses events to simulate network traffic between clients and miners. It is not particularly useful in this case, but is required boilerplate code.)

Once the logger is initialized, the startServer method (lines 18–29) will start listening for incoming TCP/IP connections on the specified port. When a message is received (line 21), the message is converted to a string (line 22) and the logging level and the message are extracted from the string (lines 23–24). This information is then used to invoke the log method of the logger class.

Most of SpartanGold's standard classes work well for our implementation. However, we extend SpartanGold's Miner class to make LoggingMiner. Two changes are worthy of closer attention.

The startNewSearch method is called whenever a search for a new block proof begins. Its responsibility is to create the block of transactions and intialize the proof field so that the proof-of-work search can begin. We extend this method to add a special transaction with the timestamp of the block. The constant BLOCK_TIME_LEVEL is set to 5, matching the BLOCK_TIME constant defined in the logging class. (As we shall see in Sect. 4.2, this method also gives us a good hook to introduce a delay in block production, simulating an attack on the log.)

---

[3]   https://logging.apache.org/log4j/2.x/.

[4]   The miner's initial balance of coins (line 40) is required; since no coins are used in transactions, the specific balance is not particularly important.

```
1    "use strict";
2
3    const net = require('net');
4    const { Blockchain, Block, Client, Transaction, FakeNet } =
5        require('spartan-gold');
6    const LoggingMiner = require('./logging-miner');
7
8    const DEBUG = 0; const INFO = 1; const WARN = 2;
9    const ERROR = 3; const FATAL = 4; const BLOCK_TIME = 5;
10
11   module.exports = class Logger {
12
13     constructor({level=WARN, powLeadingZeroes} = {}) {
14       this.level = level;
15       this.initializeBlockchain(powLeadingZeroes);
16     }
17
18     startServer(port) {
19       let srvr = net.createServer();
20       srvr.on('connection', (client) => {
21         client.on('data', (data) => {
22           let ds = data.toString();
23           let lvl = parseInt(ds.charAt(0));
24           let msg = ds.slice(1),
25           this.log(lvl, msg);
26         });
27       });
28       srvr.listen(port);
29     }
30
31     initializeBlockchain(powLeadingZeroes) {
32       let fakeNet = new FakeNet();
33       this.miner = new LoggingMiner({name: "BlockLogger", net: fakeNet});
34
35       Blockchain.makeGenesis({
36         blockClass: Block,
37         transactionClass: Transaction,
38         powLeadingZeroes: powLeadingZeroes,
39         clientBalanceMap: new Map([
40           [this.miner, 10000],
41         ]),
42       });
43       fakeNet.register(this.miner);
44
45       this.miner.initialize();
46     }
47
48     log(level, message) {
49       this.miner.postLoggingTransaction(level, message);
50     }
51
52     debug(message) {
53       this.log(DEBUG, message);
54     }
55
56     info(message) {
57       this.log(INFO, message);
58     }
59
60     warn(message) {
61       this.log(WARN, message);
62     }
63
64     error(message) {
65       this.log(ERROR, message);
66     }
67
68     fatal(message) {
69       this.log(FATAL, message);
70     }
71   }
```

Fig. 1. Logger class

The code for the `startNewSearch` method is shown below:

```
startNewSearch(txSet=new Set()) {
  super.startNewSearch(txSet);
  let tx = Blockchain.makeTransaction({
    from: this.address,
    nonce: this.nonce++,
    pubKey: this.keyPair.public,
    outputs: [],
    data: {
      level: BLOCK_TIME_LEVEL,
      time: Date.now(),
    },
  });
  tx.sign(this.keyPair.private);
  this.currentBlock.addTransaction(tx);
}
```

The `postLoggingTransaction` method sends a transaction to the miner for inclusion in the blockchain. It calls `postGenericTransaction` from its parent class, which handles many of the banal details about posting the transaction. Since we do not care about coins for these transactions, the `ouputs` field specifying who gets paid is empty, and the `fee` of coins to pay the miner for including this transaction is set to 0.

The `data` field of a SpartanGold transaction is deliberately unspecified to allow for greater ease in expanding the code. In our case, we include the level of the log, the message, and the timestamp.

The method is shown below:

```
postLoggingTransaction(level, message) {
  this.postGenericTransaction({
    outputs: [],
    fee: 0,
    data: {
      level: level,
      message: message,
      time: Date.now(),
    }
  });
}
```

3.3 Extensions

Our design uses a blockchain locally for storing messages. Given the blockchain's utility in decentralized systems, incorporating multiple servers is a natural extension.

Instead of sending transactions to a single miner, it would be straightforward to send the transactions to a network of machines, allowing them to come to consensus through the usual mining process. This approach might be useful in a company with a large network of machines.

Alternately, a smaller company might write their logs to an external blockchain. This approach might raise concerns if the logs contain any confidential data. Additionally, the cost of blockchain storage might be prohibitive.

Instead, if the logger periodically writes the hash of the latest block to the external blockchain, then we can detect any tampering of the local log file. However, it would not be possible to recreate the original logging data with this approach.

4 Experimental Results

To validate our design, we have generated a series of blockchains to serve as our dataset of untampered blockchains (that is, blockchains whose production of blocks has been continuous). In Sect. 4.2 we then show how an attempt to change a block is likely to be detected, especially if a substantial portion of blocks must be rewritten to maintain the internal consistency of the blockchain data structure.

A more subtle attacker might try to adjust the times of blocks to hide the change. In Sect. 4.3 we show how this attack may still be detected unless the attacker is able to keep the change in block times very minimal; we note that keeping the block production timestamps within this level slows down how quickly the new blockchain could be forged, and thus gives administrators more time to recognize the discrepancy. All code and data samples are available at https://github.com/taustin/hardenedLogger.

4.1 Untampered Blockchain Dataset

To generate a sample untampered blockchain, we ran SpartanGold with one message per block until 1000 blocks were created. We repeated this process 30 times to create our dataset of untampered blockchains. The dataset was generated on a MacBook Pro with an Apple M1 Pro chip with 10 cores, 16 GBs of memory, and running OSX V.12.4. We used SpartanGold v. 1.0.7. The proof-of-work target was fixed at 19 leading zeroes (binary).

Each block was printed in JavaScript Object Notation (JSON). A sample block is shown below, modified for readability:

```
{
  "000001e2b8ae0d44446bafd9564c0733f0ce1ea0b4f732ead2cd06ae22619968": {
    "chainLength": 4,
    "timestamp": 1655527429332,
    "transactions": [
      [
        "11f44ef63467c34abe83443d2093712d7871ad42646eb5f7a9defdd1bd354d8f",
        {
          "from": "Mw3+gRGVyOOaG9yWlL3bGHNSaFEkLTEmLE8xtoe4i2g=",
          "nonce": 3,
```

```
        "pubKey": "-----BEGIN PUBLIC KEY-----\nMFwwDQYJKoZIhvcNAQEBBQ...",
        "sig": "d1b095ca774163c09f98d4c3cd0de7961dc45a3487aa06d9d3092...",
        "fee": 0,
        "outputs": [],
        "data": {
            "level": 5,
            "time": 1655527429332
        }
      }
    ]
  ],
  "prevBlockHash": "00000543b2808fa8495ee488288a4f1b4731029e0b70ca994...",
  "proof": 923677,
  "rewardAddr": "Mw3+gRGVyOOaG9yWlL3bGHNSaFEkLTEmLE8xtoe4i2g="
 }
}
```

The first hash is the block ID. Similar to Bitcoin, the IDs are generated in the search for a valid proof-of-work; as a result, these IDs always begin with several leading zeroes.

The timestamp field identifies when the search for a proof-of-work for the block began. Contrasting this value with the timestamp of the next block indicates the total time that was required to find a valid proof.

In SpartanGold, the proof-of-work is discovered by initializing the proof field to 0 and then incrementing that field until the hash value meets the proof-of-work target. Since we search through the space of proofs sequentially, there should be a positive correlation between the proof and the duration needed to find the block. Of course, an attacker would not have to follow this rule and could search the space of possible proofs in any order that they desired.

Table 1 shows the average time to produce a block and the standard deviation for all of the sample blockchains in our untampered dataset. Results are reported with a precision of 5 digits.

4.2 Simple Attack

For our first experiment, we simulate an unsophisticated attack where the intruder attempts to rewrite a portion of the blockchain and continue the logs from that branch of the blockchain.

To simulate this attack, we introduced a pause at a randomly selected block before the block production was allowed to continue. As with our benign dataset, we produced 1000 blocks for each blockchain sample. For each of these blockchains, a block in the range of 25–975 was selected randomly for the delay. Other applications and system processes were allowed to run, simulating a realistic environment.

When the LoggingMiner class constructor is initialized, we specify the field compromisedBlockNumber to indicate which block should be delayed; the duration of the delay is specified in the compromiseDuration field. At the beginning

Table 1. Block production time

Filename	Average block time	Standard deviation
blockchain01.json	2706.9 ms	11560 ms
blockchain02.json	2265.3 ms	2258.1 ms
blockchain03.json	2286.6 ms	2153.1 ms
blockchain04.json	8535.3 ms	71270 ms
blockchain05.json	7088.5 ms	61485 ms
blockchain06.json	4927.2 ms	40207 ms
blockchain07.json	5134.8 ms	52046 ms
blockchain08.json	4601.6 ms	44676 ms
blockchain09.json	3733.5 ms	32390 ms
blockchain10.json	3121.5 ms	30224 ms
blockchain11.json	5958.3 ms	57157 ms
blockchain12.json	2322.9 ms	2378.4 ms
blockchain13.json	5115.6 ms	51169 ms
blockchain14.json	2237.8 ms	2134.1 ms
blockchain15.json	6853.3 ms	66749 ms
blockchain16.json	6074.8 ms	57827 ms
blockchain17.json	2242.8 ms	2170.0 ms
blockchain18.json	6100.8 ms	60305 ms
blockchain19.json	2231.5 ms	2197.9 ms
blockchain20.json	9360.7 ms	83588 ms
blockchain21.json	2324.6 ms	2432.3 ms
blockchain22.json	6999.8 ms	65890 ms
blockchain23.json	6224.8 ms	60495 ms
blockchain24.json	2348.0 ms	2299.4 ms
blockchain25.json	4669.7 ms	45306 ms
blockchain26.json	2266.0 ms	2452.6 ms
blockchain27.json	7160.8 ms	67987 ms
blockchain28.json	4129.9 ms	41964 ms
blockchain29.json	2257.5 ms	2252.5 ms
blockchain30.json	3104.3 ms	25419 ms
TOTAL	4479.5 ms	44271 ms

of the `startNewSearch` method, we introduce a check to see if the search should be delayed; if so, `setTimeout` is called to reinvoke the method after the delay. The `compromisedBlockNumber` is then deleted to allow the new call to continue as normal, and we return from the method to prevent the search from beginning earlier. After this check, the method runs as per normal. The code is shown below:

```
startNewSearch(txSet=new Set()) {
  if (!!this.currentBlock && this.compromisedBlockNumber ===
      this.currentBlock.chainLength) {
    setTimeout(() => {
      this.startNewSearch(txSet);
    }, this.compromiseDuration);

    // After compromise, the blockchain continues normally.
    delete this.compromisedBlockNumber;
    return;
  }

  super.startNewSearch(txSet);

  // The rest of this method is elided for brevity.
  ...
}
```

When the delay was set to 5 min, the compromised block took the greatest amount of time in two cases, and was among the 3 slowest blocks to be produced in all cases. The results for a five-minute delay are summarized below.

File	Time to mine block	Order (out of 1000)
blockchain-rewritten1-05.json	301414 ms	3rd
blockchain-rewritten2-05.json	302700 ms	1st
blockchain-rewritten3-05.json	301815 ms	1st
blockchain-rewritten4-05.json	303038 ms	3rd
blockchain-rewritten5-05.json	305717 ms	2nd

We can improve the results by making the logging process a higher priority. When we use the Unix nice command with a priority of -10^5, the compromised block is the slowest to be produced in all but one of our test cases, as shown below.

File	Time to mine block	Order (out of 1000)
blockchain-rewritten1-05-HP.json	300339 ms	1st
blockchain-rewritten2-05-HP.json	306931 ms	1st
blockchain-rewritten3-05-HP.json	302706 ms	1st
blockchain-rewritten4-05-HP.json	302156 ms	2nd
blockchain-rewritten5-05-HP.json	305554 ms	1st

We note that 5 min is also relatively recent activity. The deeper the change is in the blockchain, the more likely it is that this attack would be detected. These

---

[5] With the nice command, 0 is a normal priority task, 20 is the lowest priority, and -20 is the highest priority.

analyses do not attempt to account for the nonces, which would be positively correlated with the proof-of-work. It also does not account for other activity on the system. More careful analysis could consider these factors.

4.3   Subtle Attack

When the attacker attempts to recreate the blockchain by interrupting the creation of a block for a fixed amount of time, the machine learning model is immediately able to recognize the discrepancy between the block ID and the amount of time required to compute it. The detection rate, in this case, reaches an accuracy close to 100%. The attacker needs a more subtle approach. Instead of adding a fixed pause before computing new blocks, we introduce a pause that lasts a different amount of time for each block. To simulate this, we modified the timestamp of every recreated block by adding to the timestamp of the previous block a random value selected from a specified range and, then, using this as the timestamp of the current block. Note that the new timestamp cannot be less than the timestamp of the previous block, that is, the new timestamp and the previous one differ a specified number of milliseconds between 1 to the upper bound of the range. For example, the attacker pauses the process for a random number of milliseconds taken from the range 1 to 60000 (one min). In this way, the model processes timestamp differences, that is, the distance between the current timestamp's block and the previous one, that are not fixed and that vary randomly each time to imitate a more realistic scenario.

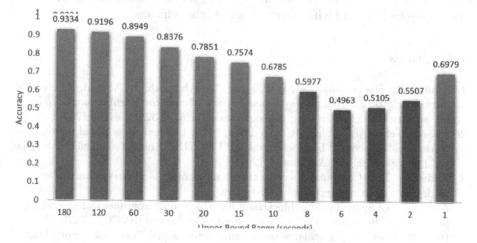

Fig. 2. Accuracy of the machine learning model for different values of the upper bound.

In Fig. 2, we see the results of this experiment while varying the upper bound of the range from which the number of milliseconds are selected (from 1 to 180 s). We notice that, when the ranges are close to the legitimate average of the timestamp's distances, the detection of a compromised block becomes unreliable. This range is highlighted in red and is comprised between 2 and 8 s.

5   Discussion and Future Work

In this paper, we have shown how a logger with a local blockchain can be used to detect log tampering. We have shown that a simple attack that only restarts the blockchain log from a given block is easily detected, and a more subtle attacker can only succeed by moving slowly, and thus opening themselves to a longer window of detection while they rewrite the blockchain.

While we have focused on a single miner, we could easily expand the system to write to multiple mining processes, or even to broadcast out to external blockchain networks. which would strengthen the defenses of the log. An interesting future direction of this research is to do so in a way that uses external blockchains to strengthen the log's defenses, but can do so in a cost-effective manner.

We are also interested in further understanding the types of attacks that the attacker could perform, and to further study detection techniques capable of identifying these attacks.

Increased accuracy in detection could be achieved by applying different machine learning techniques such as Profile Hidden Markov Models and Ensemble Learning. The model could be trained on sequences of blocks' information to increase the ability to detect tampering. Furthermore, the hash ID can be combined with additional block information to find the best combination of training inputs to achieve both higher accuracy and higher efficiency.

References

1. Ahmad, Z., Shahid Khan, A., Wai Shiang, C., Abdullah, J., Ahmad, F.: Network intrusion detection system: a systematic study of machine learning and deep learning approaches. Trans. Emerg. Telecommun. Technol. **32**(1), e4150 (2021)
2. Ali, M., Nelson, J.C., Shea, R., Freedman, M.J.: Blockstack: a global naming and storage system secured by blockchains. In: USENIX Annual Technical Conference, pp. 181–194. USENIX Association (2016)
3. Anderson, J.P.: Computer security threat monitoring and surveillance. James P. Anderson Company, Technical report (1980)
4. Austin, T.H.: Spartangold: a blockchain for education, experimentation, and rapid prototyping. In: Silicon Valley Cybersecurity Conference (SVCC) (2020)
5. Back, A.: Hashcash - a denial of service counter-measure, Technical report. http://www.hashcash.org/papers/hashcash.pdf (2002)
6. Chen, F., Wan, H., Cai, H., Cheng, G.: Machine learning in/for blockchain: future and challenges. Can. J. Stat. **49**(4), 1364–1382 (2021)
7. Chen, J., Gorbunov, S., Micali, S., Vlachos, G.: Algorand agreement: super fast and partition resilient byzantine agreement. IACR Cryptol. ePrint Arch. **2018**, 377 (2018)

8. Chen, X., Ji, J., Luo, C., Liao, W., Li, P.: When machine learning meets blockchain: a decentralized, privacy-preserving and secure design. In: 2018 IEEE International Conference on Big Data (Big Data), pp. 1178–1187. IEEE (2018)
9. Dong, B., Wang, X.: Comparison deep learning method to traditional methods using for network intrusion detection. In: 2016 8th IEEE International Conference on Communication Software and Networks (ICCSN), pp. 581–585. IEEE (2016)
10. Filecoin: A decentralized storage network. Technical report, Protocol Labs (2017)
11. Goodman, L.: Tezos - a self-amending crypto-ledger. Technical report, Tezos Foundation (2014)
12. Hanke, T., Movahedi, M., Williams, D.: DFINITY technology overview series, consensus system. CoRR abs/1805.04548 (2018). http://arxiv.org/abs/1805.04548
13. Huang, E., Di Troia, F., Stamp, M.: Evaluating deep learning models and adversarial attacks on accelerometer-based gesture authentication. arXiv preprint arXiv:2110.14597 (2021)
14. Khan, A.A., Khan, M.M., Khan, K.M., Arshad, J., Ahmad, F.: A blockchain-based decentralized machine learning framework for collaborative intrusion detection within UAVs. Comput. Netw. **196**, 108217 (2021)
15. Kiayias, A., Russell, A., David, B., Oliynykov, R.: Ouroboros: a provably secure proof-of-stake blockchain protocol. In: Advances in Cryptology - CRYPTO 2017– 37th Annual International Cryptology Conference, Proceedings, Part I, pp. 357– 388 (2017)
16. King, S.: Primecoin: Cryptocurrency with prime number proof-of-work. http://primecoin.org/static/primecoin-paper.pdf (2013)
17. King, S., Nadal, S.: Ppcoin: Peer-to-peer crypto-currency with proof-of-stake. http://primecoin.org/static/primecoin-paper.pdf (2012)
18. Lamport, L.: Paxos made simple, fast, and byzantine. In: Procedings of the International Conference on Principles of Distributed Systems. OPODIS, vol. 3, pp. 7–9. Suger, Saint-Denis, rue Catulienne, France (2002)
19. Liu, Y., Yu, F.R., Li, X., Ji, H., Leung, V.C.: Blockchain and machine learning for communications and networking systems. IEEE Commun. Surv. Tutorials **22**(2), 1392–1431 (2020)
20. Merkle, R.C.: Protocols for public key cryptosystems. In: 1980 IEEE Symposium on Security and Privacy, pp. 122–122 (1980)
21. Merrill, P., Austin, T.H., Thakker, J., Park, Y., Rietz, J.: Lock and load: a model for free blockchain transactions through token locking. In: IEEE International Conference on Decentralized Applications and Infrastructures (DAPPCON). IEEE (2019)
22. Miller, A., Juels, A., Shi, E., Parno, B., Katz, J.: Permacoin: repurposing bitcoin work for data preservation. In: IEEE Symposium on Security and Privacy, pp. 475–490. IEEE (2014)
23. Nakamoto, S.: Bitcoin: A peer-to-peer electronic cash system (2008). https://bitcoin.org/bitcoin.pdf. Accessed XX Oct 20XX
24. Namecoin homepage. https://namecoin.org/. Accessed June 2022
25. Park, S., Pietrzak, K., Kwon, A., Alwen, J., Fuchsbauer, G., Gazi, P.: Spacemint: a cryptocurrency based on proofs of space. IACR Cryptol. ePrint Arch. **2015**, 528 (2015)
26. Saber, A., Di Troia, F., Stamp, M.: Intrusion detection and CAN vehicle networks. In: Montasari, R., Jahankhani, H., Hill, R., Parkinson, S. (eds.) Digital Forensic Investigation of Internet of Things (IoT) Devices. ASTSA, pp. 125–154. Springer, Cham (2021). https://doi.org/10.1007/978-3-030-60425-7_5
27. Storj: A decentralized cloud storage network framework. Technical report, Storj Labs Inc. (2018)

28. Tendermint documentation. https://tendermint.com/docs/tendermint-core/running-in-production.html#dos-exposure-and-mitigation (2018)
29. Vorick, D., Champine, L.: Sia: Simple decentralized storage. Nebulous Inc, Technical report (2014)
30. Wood, G.: Ethereum: a secure decentralised generalised transaction ledger. https://gavwood.com/paper.pdf (2014)

Remote Device Assessment

Impact of Location Spoofing Attacks on Performance Prediction in Mobile Networks

Nikhil Sai Kanuri[1], Sang-Yoon Chang[2], Younghee Park[3], Jonghyun Kim[4], and Jinoh Kim[1]([⊠])(iD)

[1] Texas A&M University, Commerce, TX 75428, USA
jinoh.kim@tamuc.edu
[2] University of Colorado, Colorado Springs, CO 80918, USA
[3] San Jose State University, San Jose, CA 95192, USA
[4] ETRI, Yuseong, Daejeon 34129, Korea

Abstract. Performance prediction in wireless mobile networks is essential for diverse purposes in network management and operation. Particularly, the position of mobile devices is crucial to estimating the performance in the mobile communication setting. With its importance, this paper investigates mobile communication performance based on the coordinate information of mobile devices. We analyze a recent 5G data collection and examine the feasibility of location-based performance prediction. As location information is key to performance prediction, the basic assumption of making a relevant prediction is the correctness of the coordinate information of devices given. With its criticality, this paper also investigates the impact of position falsification on the ML-based performance predictor, which reveals the significant degradation of the prediction performance under such attacks, suggesting the need for effective defense mechanisms against location spoofing threats.

Keywords: Performance prediction · Location spoofing · Position falsification · Mobile networks · Machine learning

1 Introduction

Performance prediction in wireless mobile networks is essential for network optimization and management [8], application offloading decisions [10], deployment of unmanned aerial vehicles (UAVs) also known as flying base stations [3], to list a few. In fact, there would be different angles on performance prediction in mobile communication, from low-level channel performance [11,12] to mobile application/device throughput [6,8,10]. In this study, we focus on application throughput of mobile devices for predicting and evaluating.

In the mobile communication setting, the position of mobile devices is significantly crucial to estimate the performance. Simply speaking, even for a single mobile device, the measured performance of that device may show a high degree

© The Author(s) 2022
L. Bathen et al. (Eds.): SVCC 2022, CCIS 1683, pp. 107–119, 2022.
https://doi.org/10.1007/978-3-031-24049-2_7

of fluctuation depending on its location (e.g., due to the density of devices, signal strength, and interference/reflection). In this study, we investigate mobile communication performance based on the coordinate information of mobile devices. We analyze a recent 5G data collection [7], which contains a set of features including the GPS coordinates, velocity, and application throughput information of mobile devices, with a machine learning (ML) approach.

As the location information is key to performance prediction, the basic assumption of making relevant prediction is the correctness of the coordinate information of devices given. However, any malfunctioning of location chips (e.g., receiving GPS signals) may result in an unacceptably erroneous estimation (although rare). A more common scenario is location spoofing taken place intentionally; that is, a location spoofing attack falsifying the position information can be attempted with a malicious intent, which is one of the greatest security concerns in mobile communication networks [4, 9]. With its criticality, this paper investigates the impact of position falsification on the presented ML-based performance predictor.

While this paper presents our initial experimental results and observations, there are several contributions non-trivial to the research community. Firstly, this paper examines the feasibility of location-based performance prediction. An interesting observation is that it is possible to estimate application throughput with 80% accuracy using a small set of features readily available when establishing the communication channel. Secondly, the impact of location-spoofing attacks on performance prediction is evaluated, with the intuition that location-based performance prediction would be critical to such threats. The experimental result shows a significant degradation of the performance prediction quality, signaling the need for effective defense mechanisms against location-spoofing attacks to enable reliable estimations.

The organization of this paper is as follows. We first introduce the 5G dataset employed for performance prediction in Sect. 2, with exploratory data analysis. In Sect. 3, location-based performance prediction is discussed with our initial experimental results for binary and multi-class classifications. Section 4 shows the impact of location spoofing attacks on performance prediction using two types of position falsification techniques (constant and constant-offset spoofing). Section 5 provides a summary of closely related studies, and we conclude our presentation with future research directions in Sect. 6.

2   Exploratory Analysis of 5G Dataset

This study employs a recent 5G dataset collected from an Irish mobile operator network [7]. The data collection was made using different file access applications, including file transfer and video streaming. The throughput of such applications was measured in different locations and mobility options (stationary or driving), in addition to other channel and context information. The number of features defined in this dataset is 26 features in total. Table 1 provides the features referred to for our performance prediction study.

Table 1. Selected features defined in the 5G dataset

Feature	Description
Longitude	GPS longitude of mobile device
Latitude	GPS latitude of mobile device
Velocity	Speed of mobile device (in Km/h)
SNR	Signal-to-noise ratio (dB)
RSRP	Reference signal received power
RSSI	Received signal strength indicator
RSRQ	Reference signal received quality (a ratio between RSRP and RSSI)
CQI	Channel quality indicator
State	Downloading or Idle
DL_bitrate (Tput)	Application-level download throughput (in Kbps)

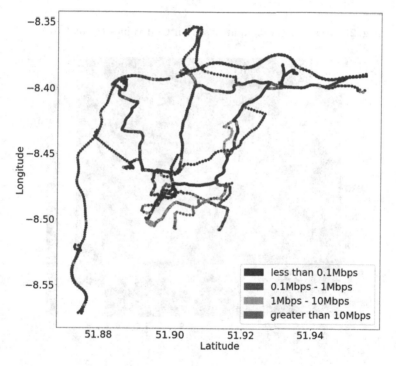

Fig. 1. Throughput map based on the measurement, showing the feasibility of estimating throughput based on the coordinate of the mobile device. (Color figure online)

The number of samples is roughly 189K in the raw dataset. From the original dataset, we remove data instances meeting any of the following conditions: (i) DL_bitrate=0, (ii) State=Idle, and (iii) if any feature contains a null value. Note that the State feature defines the state of the download process, whether it is downloading or idle (i.e., not downloading). After this removal process, the pre-processed dataset contains 81,859 instances in total.

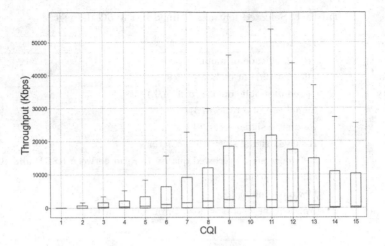

Fig. 2. Measured throughput based on CQI values (from 1 to 15)

	Longitude	Latitude	Speed	RSRP	RSRQ	SNR	CQI	RSSI	DL_bitrate
Longitude	1	0.027	-0.17	-0.48	-0.073	0.11	0.24	-0.47	0.17
Latitude	0.027	1	0.54	0.16	0.37	0.25	0.15	0.25	-0.24
Speed	-0.17	0.54	1	0.25	0.28	0.15	-0.014	0.27	-0.16
RSRP	-0.48	0.16	0.25	1	0.38	0.41	0.25	0.7	-0.045
RSRQ	-0.073	0.37	0.28	0.38	1	0.58	0.32	0.34	-0.14
SNR	0.11	0.25	0.15	0.41	0.58	1	0.44	0.28	0.016
CQI	0.24	0.15	-0.014	0.25	0.32	0.44	1	0.17	0.027
RSSI	-0.47	0.25	0.27	0.7	0.34	0.28	0.17	1	-0.29
DL_bitrate	0.17	-0.24	-0.16	-0.045	-0.14	0.016	0.027	-0.29	1

Fig. 3. Correlation matrix of the selected features (positive correlation → +1, negative correlation → −1, less correlation → 0)

We carried out initial explorations to understand potential correlations of the features in the throughput feature (Tput). Figure 1 shows the throughput information on the coordinate space. The figure shows four different throughput ranges: (i) Tput < 100 Kbps, (ii) 100 Kbps ≤ Tput < 1 Mbps, (iii) 1 Mbps ≤ Tput < 10 Mbps, and (iv) Tput ≥ 10 Mbps. From the figure, we can see

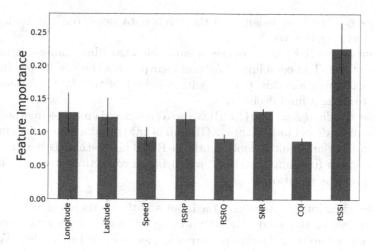

Fig. 4. Feature importance (compiled by random forest): None of the features works dominantly for predicting throughput (DL_bitrate).

that the location information would be helpful for estimating throughput. While some spots (colored in red or orange) show a relatively greater throughput, the rest (in blue or dark blue) show quite low bit rates. The figure also reveals some clusters having higher throughput.

The box plot in Fig. 2 provides the measured throughput over different CQI values. The CQI of a mobile device is a feedback indicating the channel data rate, provided to the base station (eNB). A previous study in [7] reported a partially proportional pattern between CQI and throughput. Our experimental result does not show such proportionality clearly; rather it shows different throughput ranges for each CQI value.

To see how the features are correlated with each other, Fig. 3 provides a correlation matrix. We can see that the feature of RSRP is strongly correlated to RSSI, while RSRP is also somewhat correlated to SNR. Additionally, the feature of RSRQ shows a high degree of correlation with SNR. For the throughput feature (DL_bitrate), none of the features shows any strong correlation. In the next section, we will examine the feasibility of throughput prediction using conventional ML methods. In addition, Fig. 4 shows the importance of the features to determine throughput, compiled by using a random forest classifier (described in Sect. 3). While RSSI is important the most, the result shows any of the features does not play dominantly for predicting throughput.

3   Performance Prediction

In this study, we reduce the performance prediction to a classification problem. We employ several conventional supervised learning methods for making the classification, as follows:

- *k-Nearest Neighbors* (KNN) performs the grouping of data samples based on the proximity information. To classify, the class label most frequently found from its neighbors is assigned to the given data point (on the basis of the concept of majority vote).

– *Random Forest* (RF) is a tree-based ensemble algorithm combining multiple decision trees. The combining function incorporates the results produced by individual tree trained in parallel with a subset of the data randomly allocated, to make a final decision.

– *Extreme Gradient Boosting* (XGB) is also a tree-based ensemble method based on a gradient descent algorithm. XGB builds one tree at a time, while multiple decision trees are built independently in RF. This method is based on minimizing a loss function iteratively, which is the correction of errors observed in the previous iteration.

The classification problem takes the input and the predicted class is produced as the outcome. In this study, we set up three different feature sets to evaluate their impact on the classification performance, as described in Table 2. We basically perform the performance prediction based on the position information. For Set-1, it is reasonable to assume the velocity information is available when issuing the prediction request, whereas the other features defined in Table 1 might not be available before making the actual communication. Figure 2 shows the correlation between CQI and throughput (although not strong), and Set-2 refers to the CQI value in addition to the basic Set-1 features. Lastly, Set-3 refers to the entire feature set defined in Table 2 except State and Tput.

Table 2. Evaluated feature sets for performance prediction

Set	Features
Set-1	{Longitude, Latitude, Velocity} (*default*)
Set-2	{Longitude, Latitude, Velocity, CQI}
Set-3	{Longitude, Latitude, Velocity, CQI, SNR, RSRP, RSSI, RSRQ}

For actual evaluation, we partition the dataset into two disjoint sets for training (70%) and testing (30%). To report classification performance, we consider two standard measures of Accuracy and F1-score: Accuracy is a fraction of the correctly classified samples, while F1-score is a harmonic mean and balanced in case of an unbalanced class distribution (i.e., majority vs. minority classes). To consider a class imbalance concern in the evaluation settings, we mainly utilize F1 score by default, unless otherwise mentioned.

3.1 Binary Classification Performance

We first evaluate the binary classification performance. Two classes are defined as: *low* if tput ≤ 1 Mbps; *high* otherwise, in a balanced manner with respect to the distribution of data instances. The Class-0 (low) contains 39,730 samples (48.5%) and the Class-1 (high) does 42,129 samples (51.5%).

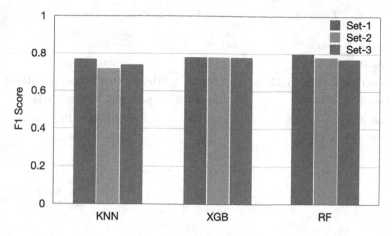

Fig. 5. Binary class classification performance: RF performs the best with Set-1, while XGB performs consistently over different feature sets.

Figure 5 shows the prediction performance in F1 score. The evaluation result shows that RF yields the greatest performance, while XGB shows the consistent performance over the reliance on different feature sets. The KNN algorithm shows slightly lower performance than the other two schemes. Note that we set $k = 11$ that produces the best performance for KNN (between 1 and 100 for the k value), while we simply take the default setting for RF and XGB (without intensive optimizations).

An interesting observation is that referencing additional features would *not* be helpful for improving the prediction performance. In fact, all the classifiers show that using set-1 performs better than or at least equal to the use of other feature sets. We conjecture that this is because any feature defined in Set-2 and Set-3 has no strong correlation to the throughput feature, as depicted in the correlation matrix in Fig. 3. The result here shows that the position information plays a significant role for estimating throughput, and this is somewhat intuitive since a mobile device may show a high degree of fluctuation in application throughput depending on its location due to several reasons, such as the density of devices, signal strength, and interference/reflection.

It is important to note that the features in Set-1 are readily available when establishing actual communication channels, and it is possible to estimate application performance (throughput) with 80% accuracy (precisely F1 score) using the RF predictor. In contrast, the features additionally defined in Set-2 and Set-3 may *not* be available beforehand at the connection set-up time.

Table 3. Class definition for multi-class prediction

Classes	3-class	4-class	5-class
Class-0	<0.1 Mbps	<0.1 Mbps	<0.01 Mbps
Class-1	[0.1 Mbps, 1 Mbps)	[0.1 Mbps, 1 Mbps)	[0.01 Mbps, 0.1 Mbps)
Class-2	≥1Mbps	[1 Mbps, 10 Mbps)	[0.1 Mbps, 1 Mbps)
Class-3	–	≥10 Mbps	[1 Mbps, 10 Mbps)
Class-4	–	–	≥10 Mbps

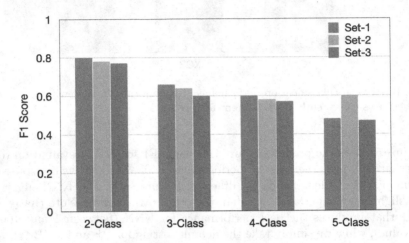

Fig. 6. Multi-class prediction performance (RF): Defining a more number of classes results in the significant degradation of the estimation performance.

3.2 Multi-class Prediction Performance

We also examine the performance prediction tools with multi-class classification settings. Table 3 shows the class definition, for 3-class, 4-class, and 5-class classification settings.

Figure 6 shows the multi-class classification performance for RF. For the comparison purpose, the figure includes the binary classification result as well, As expected, defining a more number of classes results in the significant degradation of the estimation performance. For 3-class classification, the performance goes down to 62% (from 80% when performing the binary classification). As in the binary classification, the multi-class prediction result also shows using Set-1 performs better than using the other feature sets.

The other two classifiers (KNN and XGB) also showed the similar pattern, with slightly lower performance than RF. Figure 7 shows the multi-class prediction result for different classifiers when using Set-1. We can see that RF shows the best performance consistently, while XGB performs better than KNN.

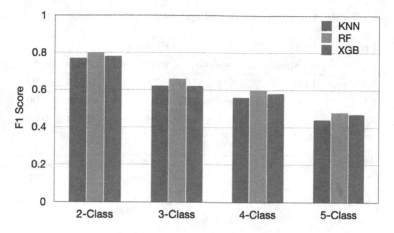

Fig. 7. Multi-class prediction performance (Set-1): RF shows the best performance consistently, while XGB performs better than KNN.

4 Location Spoofing Attacks

We next investigate the impact of location-spoofing attacks on the coordinate-based performance prediction. In fact, location-spoofing attacks are one of the critical attacks in mobile communication environments. A widely-used Vehicular Ad-hoc Networks (VANETs) dataset, VeReMi, assumes five different types for location spoofing attacks [2]: (i) *Constant* attack transmitting a pre-defined coordinate, (ii) *Constant offset* adding a pre-defined offset to the original coordinate, (iii) *Random* transmitting a random coordinate, (iv) *Random offset* providing a random coordinate in a predefined rectangle around the original coordinate, and (v) Eventual stop transmitting the current coordinate without any change (although moving).

In this study, we evaluate the impact of spoofing attacks with constant spoofing and constant offset spoofing. Again, the *constant spoofing* attack overwrites the location information with the constant value. We chose five random positions to simulate the constant spoofing attack (within the coordinate space). The second scenario is the use of constant offset attack, in which a constant offset value is added to the original coordinate. For the constant offset attack, we use the notion of *perturbation degree*: In the coordinate space in the 5G dataset, it is straightforward to calculate the width of latitude space (i.e., $|x| = x_{max} - x_{min}$) and the height of the longitude space ($|y| = y_{max} - y_{min}$). The constant offset for a perturbation degree p is defined as $p \times (|x|, |y|)$. For the constant offset attack, we configure different perturbation degrees from 5% to 50% to define the offset.

Table 4 shows the performance prediction result with and without spoofing attacks. The experiment was performed with Set-1 for the binary prediction. Since five different coordinates were randomly picked up, we report the result with the average and standard deviation (for w/ spoofing). As can be seen from

Table 4. Impact of constant spoofing attack (with Set-1)

Predictor	Average		F1 score	
	wo/spoofing	w/spoofing	wo/spoofing	w/spoofing
KNN	0.77	0.524 ± 0.02	0.77	0.486 ± 0.08
RF	0.77	0.502 ± 0.02	0.80	0.342 ± 0.00
XGB	0.78	0.504 ± 0.01	0.78	0.344 ± 0.01

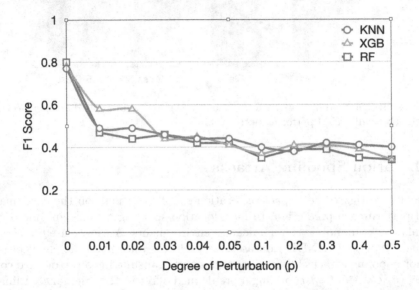

Fig. 8. Impact of constant offset spoofing attacks on performance prediction (binary classification): Even a small perturbation degree ($p = 1\%$) significantly impacts on performance prediction, from 80% to lower than 60% in F1 score, regardless of classifier types. Note that $p = 0$ indicates no spoofing attack applied.

the table, even this simple spoofing attack considerably degrades the prediction performance. For instance, RF becomes degraded from 80% to 34.2% in F1 score, while KNN is slightly less affected than RF and XGB.

The constant spoofing attack would be easily detected and resisted as it relies on static positions. The constant offset attack is more complicated to detect since the modified coordinate is based on the original location. Figure 8 shows the binary classification performance over different perturbation degrees (p). Note that $p = 0$ indicates no spoofing attack applied. As can be seen from the figure, even a small perturbation degree ($p = 1\%$) significantly impacts on performance prediction, from 80% to lower than 60% in F1 score, regardless of classifier types. With a greater degree of perturbation, the prediction performance drops below 50% if $p \geq 3\%$ for any classifier. The result here signals the need for effective defense mechanisms against location-spoofing attacks for reliable estimation of throughput in a mobile communication setting.

5   Related Work

A recent study in [6] investigated mobile bandwidth prediction using 4G and 5G datasets. For bandwidth prediction, the authors applied a Recurrent Neural Network (RNN) structure by formulating the prediction problem as a time series forecasting. Their experimental result shows better performance than the conventional univariate and multivariate prediction models. This previous work assumes bandwidth prediction as a (continuous) regression problem, while our study defines the throughput estimation as a (discrete) classification problem.

The authors in [5] evaluated the impact of location spoofing attacks using the VeReMi dataset. In this previous work, two machine learning algorithms of KNN and Support Vector Machine (SVM) were examined. The measured detection performance against spoofing attacks shows over 99% (in recall and precision). A recent study in [1] investigated the detection of falsified positions and the corresponding attack types in vehicular communication networks using a boosting decision tree ensemble technique. Our study analyzes the 5G dataset to understand the impact of location spoofing attacks on performance prediction (rather than detection of spoofed coordinates).

6   Conclusion

This paper investigates mobile communication performance based on the coordinate information of mobile devices using an ML approach. Only using three features of <Longitude, Latitude, Velocity>, we observed up to 80% correct decisions (in F1 score) for binary prediction using a conventional random forest classifier. However, the experimental result shows the location-based performance prediction becomes considerably degraded when assuming more than two classes (i.e., multi-class prediction). This paper also investigated the impact of location-spoofing attacks on the coordinate-based performance prediction, since location-spoofing attacks are one of the critical attacks in mobile communication environments. The location spoofing attacks significantly impact on performance prediction from 80% to lower than 50% correct decisions, signaling the need for effective defense mechanisms for reliable performance estimation.

In this initial study, we employed conventional ML methods (KNN, RF, and XGB) for predicting throughput in a mobile communication setting. The observed performance of 80% for binary classification could be improved by designing more sophisticated learning models (e.g., using deep structures), which is one of the future tasks of this study. Additionally, this paper showed the significant impact of location spoofing attacks on performance prediction by applying two spoofing attack types (constant spoofing and constant offset spoofing). For more a sophisticated ML model resilient to such attack types, it will be interesting to apply other types of spoofing attacks (i.e., random, random offset, and eventual stop spoofing) for evaluating the robustness to location spoofing.

Another interesting research avenue is the investigation of defense mechanisms against potential spoofing attacks, with the impact on performance prediction.

Acknowledgment. This work was supported by Institute of Information & communications Technology Planning & Evaluation (IITP) grant funded by the Korea government (MSIT) (No.2021-0-00796, Research on Foundational Technologies for 6G Autonomous Security-by-Design to Guarantee Constant Quality of Security).

References

1. Elsayed, M.A., Zincir-Heywood, N.: BoostGuard: interpretable misbehavior detection in vehicular communication networks. In: NOMS 2022–2022 IEEE/IFIP Network Operations and Management Symposium, pp. 1–9. IEEE (2022)
2. van der Heijden, R.W., Lukaseder, T., Kargl, F.: VeReMi: a dataset for comparable evaluation of misbehavior detection in VANETs. In: Beyah, R., Chang, B., Li, Y., Zhu, S. (eds.) SecureComm 2018. LNICST, vol. 254, pp. 318–337. Springer, Cham (2018). https://doi.org/10.1007/978-3-030-01701-9_18
3. Ho, T.M., Nguyen, K.K., Cheriet, M.: UAV control for wireless service provisioning in critical demand areas: a deep reinforcement learning approach. IEEE Trans. Veh. Technol. **70**(7), 7138–7152 (2021)
4. Kamal, M., Barua, A., Vitale, C., Laoudias, C., Ellinas, G.: GPS location spoofing attack detection for enhancing the security of autonomous vehicles. In: 2021 IEEE 94th Vehicular Technology Conference (VTC2021-Fall), pp. 1–7. IEEE (2021)
5. Le, A., Maple, C.: Shadows don't lie: n-sequence trajectory inspection for misbehaviour detection and classification in VANETS. In: 2019 IEEE 90th Vehicular Technology Conference (VTC2019-Fall), pp. 1–6. IEEE (2019)
6. Mei, L., Gou, J., Cai, Y., Cao, H., Liu, Y.: Realtime mobile bandwidth and handoff predictions in 4G/5G networks. Comput. Netw. **204**, 108736 (2022)
7. Raca, D., Leahy, D., Sreenan, C.J., Quinlan, J.J.: Beyond throughput, the next generation: a 5G dataset with channel and context metrics. In: Proceedings of the 11th ACM Multimedia Systems Conference, pp. 303–308 (2020)
8. Riihijarvi, J., Mahonen, P.: Machine learning for performance prediction in mobile cellular networks. IEEE Comput. Intell. Mag. **13**(1), 51–60 (2018)
9. Sharma, A., Jaekel, A.: Machine learning approach for detecting location spoofing in vanet. In: 2021 International Conference on Computer Communications and Networks (ICCCN), pp. 1–6. IEEE (2021)
10. da Silva Pinheiro, T.F., Silva, F.A., Fé, I., Kosta, S., Maciel, P.: Performance prediction for supporting mobile applications' offloading. J. Supercomput. **74**(8), 4060–4103 (2018)
11. Xu, L., Quan, T., Wang, J., Gulliver, T.A., Le, K.N.: GR and BP neural network-based performance prediction of dual-antenna mobile communication networks. Comput. Netw. **172**, 107172 (2020)
12. Xu, L., Wang, J., Wang, H., Aaron Gulliver, T., Le, K.N.: BP neural network-based ABEP performance prediction for mobile internet of things communication systems. Neural Comput. Appl. **32**(20), 16025–16041 (2020)

Deep IoT Monitoring: Filtering IoT Traffic Using Deep Learning

Gargi Gopalkrishna Prabhugaonkar, Xiaoyan Sun$^{(\boxtimes)}$, Xuyu Wang, and Jun Dai

California State University, Sacramento, CA 95819, USA
{gprabhugaonkar,xiaoyan.sun,xuyu.wang,jun.dai}@csus.edu

Abstract. The use of IoT devices has significantly increased in recent years, but there have been growing concerns about the security and privacy issues associated with these IoT devices. A recent trend is to use deep network models to classify attack and benign traffic. A traditional approach is to train the models using centrally stored data collected from all the devices in the network. However, this framework raises concerns around data privacy and security. Attacks on the central server can compromise the data and expose sensitive information. To address the issues of data privacy and security, federated learning is now a widely studied solution in the research community. In this paper, we explore and implement federated learning techniques to detect attack traffic in the IoT network. We use Deep Neural Networks on the labeled dataset and Autoencoder on the unlabeled dataset in a federated framework. We implement different model aggregation algorithms such as FedSGD, FedAvg, and FedProx for federated learning. We compare the performance of these federated learning models with the models in a centralized framework and study which aggregation algorithm for the global model yields the best performance for detecting attack traffic in the IoT network.

1 Introduction

The global market for IoT is rapidly growing, which will rise from $250.72 billion to $1.4 trillion from 2019 to 2027 [2]. Also, the Smart Home market is expected to grow to $174 billion by 2025 from $55 billion in 2016. Currently, there are over 175 million smart homes on a global scale. Some commonly used smart home IoT devices include video-enabled door alarms, locks with remote access, device-controlled burglar alarms, face recognition systems, and many more [3]. The advantages of IoT technology include the ability to access devices remotely and automate tasks that have enhanced the overall experience in homes [1]. However, this improved communication has the risks of security exploits which may expose data to unwanted sources. This can result in potential threats to the environment in which the attacked device is located. The risk is higher when the data is collected from multiple devices. Large, combined datasets can help attackers learn patterns about the users and businesses. The security of these IoT devices and data privacy is a very important issue that needs to be addressed.

L. Bathen et al. (Eds.): SVCC 2022, CCIS 1683, pp. 120–136, 2022.
https://doi.org/10.1007/978-3-031-24049-2_8

Anomaly network intrusion detection systems, which distinguish between normal behavior and abnormal behavior, have been commonly used to detect attacks towards IoT devices. A subset of anomaly-based network intrusion detection methods use deep network models to classify attacks and benign traffic. Traditionally, machine learning models have been trained in a centralized framework by collecting and storing data at a central server. However, this approach increases security risks as data containing sensitive information can be compromised due to an attack on the central server. Other risks include vulnerability to data leaks during data transfer from individual devices to the central server.

With the increasing attention to data privacy, it is important to identify alternative solutions that can ensure the security of IoT devices while protecting data privacy. Federated learning is a promising solution to address the issues of training machine learning models within a centralized framework. It uses a global model to aggregate models trained on the devices. It helps prevent breaches of sensitive data as the data is not shared across the network for machine learning model training [4]. It eliminates the need for data collection at a central location for model training. The devices use their own local data set to train the local model. The trained model is sent to the global model for aggregation and an improved updated version of the model is downloaded to the device for training. The global model aggregates the local-device models without having the need to be trained on the entire dataset.

In this paper, we explore and implement federated learning techniques to detect attack traffic in the IoT network. We use MQTTset [5], a public dataset to train simulated devices in a federated framework. Along with benign network traffic, this dataset contains five types of attacks. We use this dataset to implement supervised and unsupervised deep learning models in a federated learning framework. For supervised deep learning we use Deep Neural Networks and for unsupervised deep learning we use Autoencoders. We implement three federated global model averaging algorithms - FedSGD, FedAvg, and FedProx and perform experiments by adjusting model training parameters. To compare the performance of federated learning with centralized learning, we also implement similar models in a centralized framework by using accuracy as a performance metric. The goal of this paper is to learn the performance of federated learning framework for detecting attacks in IoT networks by using supervised and unsupervised deep learning models, and determine which aggregation algorithm for the global model yields the best performance.

2   Our Approach

2.1   Dataset

In this paper, we use a public dataset, the MQTTset [5] which contains data from home-based IoT sensors. This dataset is also focused on the Message Queue Telemetry Transport (MQTT) protocol, which is widely used nowadays in IoT networks. To simulate the smart home environment, MQTTset includes IoT devices of different natures, such as motion sensors, humidity, and temperature. A tool called IoT Flock is used to generate network traffic in MQTTset. This tool allows the configuration of networks based on scenarios and protocol-specific threats. The network consists of eight sensors and an MQTT broker. The IoT devices are connected to this broker, and the communication uses MQTT Protocol. This data set contains legitimate traffic and attack traffic. It contains five types of attacks namely Flooding Denial of Service attack, MQTT Publish Flood attack, Slow Denial of Service in the Internet of Things environment (Slow ITe) attack, Malformed Data attack, and Brute Force Authentication attack. We grouped five types of attacks into a group labelled as attacks. Besides, the dataset contains a total of 330,926 records and 34 columns.

Data Preprocessing. The data preprocessing steps are common for centralized and federated learning. One key difference is that for supervised learning implementation we use the target column while in unsupervised learning we drop this column so that the Autoencoder is trained without any labels as expected.

For binary classification, we group and relabel the five threat types as 1 and legitimate as 0. Therefore, all benign records are marked as 0 and attacks are marked as 1. Next, since we perform categorical encoding by changing the datatypes of all records to type "category" for consistency. This results in the datatype of all data values to integer. Sklearn library [7] provides train_test_split() method to split the entire dataset into train set and test set with test size of 30%, which results in 231,648 records in the train set and 99,278 records in the test set for supervised learning. Since the Autoencoder is trained only using benign data, we use 115,814 records for unsupervised learning.

Dataset Splitting for Federated Learning. In federated learning, the data resides on the devices in the network that run machine learning models locally. For our implementation, to simulate the federated learning setup, we distribute the data locally among clients. The dataset used in our experiments has an Independent and Identical Distribution (I.I.D). Considering the nature of the dataset used, we split the MQTTset in an I.I.D manner. As the data samples in this dataset are not dependent on each other and can be distributed independently, I.I.D splitting is a natural choice. This splitting is used only for our supervised learning experiments. The dataset is split based on the target column which identifies each record as an attack or benign. However, when the data is allotted to each client, it must be distributed based on the index of the data record. We use a dictionary data structure to store the data for each client in a $<key, value>$ pair. Each client is the key, and the value is a set of data record indices assigned to the client. The data dictionary contains only data indices and actual data. So as the next step, we need to assign each client the actual data record based on the indices assigned to it. To assign the actual record we use a PyTorch data loading utility called DataLoader along with a custom class that returns actual data record based an input index. We use this data splitting technique to distribute data among each client.

2.2 Approach Overview

This section provides an overview of our approach for detecting attack traffic in IoT networks. For the federated framework, we implement both supervised and unsupervised learning to compare how the attack detection performs on labeled and unlabeled data. 1) For supervised learning, we use a deep neural network. The performance of the global model in a federated framework depends on the model averaging algorithm to improve the global model. We implement three model averaging algorithms - FedSGD, FedAvg, and FedProx. For supervised DNN in a federated framework, we implement all three algorithms to understand the differences and learn which algorithm yields the best results. 2) For unsupervised learning we use an Autoencoder. We use the FedAvg with Adam optimizer for the implementation, because it produces the best results compared to other algorithms we implemented for supervised learning.

To compare with the federated framework, we also implement supervised learning and unsupervised learning in a centralized framework. In centralized learning, we also use DNN for labeled data and Autoencoder for unlabeled data. As the global model for centralized learning is trained directly on the centralized data, there are no averaging algorithms required in this framework.

Federated learning is different from traditional centralized learning methods. In federated learning, the interaction between the server and the client occurs during the communication round. During each round, the clients only exchange models while the data resides locally on each client. The approach is depicted in Fig. 1a showing how we use federated learning in IoT networks. During the initialization phase, each client is trained locally using the MQTTset distributed among clients. The global model is initialized, which is not trained on any data. The structure of the model is same as the local models. The local model on a given client is initialized for local model training. The ways in which the clients are trained and the global model is averaged depend on the specific algorithm used in the implementation. The following steps are executed during each communication round: 1) Each client receives a copy of the global model; 2) Each client trains a local model using its local dataset over e epochs and l number of local batches; 3) At the end of the round, the updated local models are sent back to the central server, where all the models received are aggregated to update the global model, which is a better version compared to the previous round. Steps $1 - 3$ are repeated for each round as the global model learns indirectly from individual local models without exchanging any data.

The evaluation phase is depicted in Fig. 1b. In this step, we use the MQTTset test data for evaluation using the global model. The global model is improved by averaging the local client model after each round based on the algorithm. Therefore, it learns about the entire network through the averaged models. The accuracy of the model is determined based on the output value of the correct prediction.

Using unsupervised Autoencoders is based on the assumption that the attack traffic will have features different from the benign traffic. During the training phase, we train the autoencoder only on benign traffic. During the evaluation phase, the test data contains both benign and attack traffic, so the global model determines the reconstruction loss for both types of data. Our goal is to optimize the encoder by minimizing this reconstruction loss. By training the autoencoders on benign traffic data, we can identify the attack traffic during the evaluation

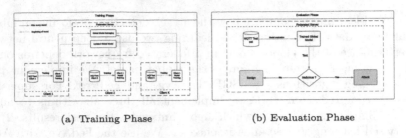

(a) Training Phase   (b) Evaluation Phase

Fig. 1. Federated training and evaluation phase

stage of the reconstruction loss. A threshold value is determined based on the reconstruction loss of the benign traffic. Using the threshold value, we can classify the traffic as benign or attack.

2.3   Federated Learning Algorithms

For supervised federated learning, we implemented three federated averaging algorithms - FedSGD, FedAvg, and FedPro for local model aggregation to improve the global model.

FedSGD. In federated learning, the global model can be improved by averaging the gradients or weights of the local client models. In the FederatedSGD (FedSGD) [8] algorithm, the model weights are updated by the Eq. 1 [8],

$$w_{new} = w_{old} - (\eta * g), \tag{1}$$

where w_{new} represents the new weights of the model, w_{old} represents the weights before update, η represents the learning rate and g are the gradients.

Specifically, for the global model, the weights are updated as described in Eq. 2 [8],

$$w_{new} = w_{old} - (\eta * (\Sigma_{k=1}^{K} \frac{n_k}{n} * g_k)), \tag{2}$$

where n represents the total number of data samples across all the clients, n_k represents the number of data samples and g_k represents the gradients on K^{th} client.

In a single epoch, the gradients do not get updated while the model weights are updated. Gradients relate to the loss function used during the epoch. Accumulation of gradients can cause two problems: the vanishing gradient problem where the gradients become too small, and the exploding gradient problem where the gradients get too large. Therefore, it is important that the gradients are cleared at the beginning of each epoch.

FedAvg. Using the FederatedAveraging Algorithm [8] (FedAvg) the global model is improved by averaging the model weights received from individual clients. A *ClientUpdate* function accepts the arguments, virtual device, and client dictionary. Each client dictionary contains the model, dataset, criterion, optimizer, and loss. The *ClientUpdate* function is run on each client to train each client on its local dataset and update these models through the client dictionary. During the training phase, the gradients are cleared, the loss between the actual and predicted values is calculated and finally, the weights are updated. At the end of *ClientUpdate* invocation, the trained model is updated in the client dictionary and returned to the global server. A model average function is then invoked to average the model weights calculated from the models trained on each client using their local dataset.

FedProx. FedProx [8] is a generalization of the FedAvg algorithm. In the FedAvg algorithm, during each round of global model update, not all clients are included for model training. Hence, not all model updates from the clients are included. This problem will affect the overall accuracy of the global model.

To improve the accuracy of the global model, the FedProx algorithm has been proposed to improve the performance of FedAvg in terms of the clients included during the global model update. Instead of excluding some clients, all the clients are trained but the number of epochs over which these clients are trained may vary across clients. We classify the clients included during each global model update round into three major groups: K = Total number of clients; S = Selected clients that during each round of global model update where $S \in K$; A = Active clients that contribute to the model averaging step where $A \in S$; R = Rest of the clients that belong to S but not A where $R \in (S - A)$.

In FedAvg, the global model averages model weights from only the active clients, while in FedProx, R clients also contribute to the model averaging steps, thus expected to improve global model accuracy, and improve in fewer communication rounds. In FedProx, we consider a proximal term which basically calculates the difference between the client model and global model. We consider the global model because it is better than the local client model at any point. The proximal term improves the overall accuracy by improving the model updates. In FedProx the weights are updated as described in Eq. 3 [9],

$$w_{new} = w_{old} - (\eta * (g + \mu(w_k - w_g))), \tag{3}$$

where μ is described as a parameter that is a re-parameterization of E [9]. The other terms w_k and w_g represent the model weights of the given client and global model weights, respectively.

3   Experiment Setup

We train and evaluate all the ML models using Google Colaboratory Pro with GPU hardware accelerator and Google Drive to store the dataset. For federated learning implementation for supervised and unsupervised learning, we simulate the setup by creating virtual clients. We use a Python library called PySyft which decouples private data from model training [10]. We use PySyft version 0.2.9 and Pytorch version 1.6. PySyft provides get() and send() methods for exchanging models between the client and server.

For supervised learning, we implement a DNN with structure summarized in Fig. 2. The activation function transforms the weighted sum of inputs into

output for the node. We also use a rectified linear activation function (ReLU).
For the output layer, we use a Sigmoid activation function which transforms the
result into a value between 0 and 1. We also use a dropout to randomly ignore
neurons during the training process to prevent the model from overfitting.

The autoencoder implemented in this paper consists of 2 fully connected layers with ReLU and Leaky ReLU activation functions. The decoder has a similar
structure where the neurons are placed in an opposite way like the structure of
the encoder. The number of neurons in the input layer of the encoder and the
output layer of the decoder is the same as expected.

```
================================================================================
==========
Layer (type:depth-idx)              Output Shape              Param #
================================================================================
==========
Net                                 --                        --
├─Linear: 1-1                       [23]                      782
├─ReLU: 1-2                         [23]                      --
├─Linear: 1-3                       [17]                      408
├─ReLU: 1-4                         [17]                      --
├─Dropout: 1-5                      [17]                      --
├─Linear: 1-6                       [1]                       18
├─Sigmoid: 1-7                      [1]                       --
================================================================================
==========
Total params: 1,208
Trainable params: 1,208
Non-trainable params: 0
Total mult-adds (M): 0.02
================================================================================
==========
Input size (MB): 0.00
Forward/backward pass size (MB): 0.00
Params size (MB): 0.00
Estimated Total Size (MB): 0.01
================================================================================
==========
```

Fig. 2. Model summary for supervised DNN

4   Experiment Results

We present the experiment results in this section. We use the following performance metrics for machine learning model evaluation. 1) Accuracy is the ratio
of correct predictions to the predictions made. As we use a balanced dataset
for our experiments, we can use accuracy as a performance metric to evaluate the model. Logarithmic Loss is used to penalizing false classifications. Low
loss results in higher accuracy of the classifier. 2) A Confusion Matrix (CM)
describes the complete model performance. It contains four important values:
true positive where both actual and predicated classification is "attack"; true
negative where both actual and predicated classification is "benign"; false positive where the actual classification is "benign" but the predicted classification is
"attack"; and false negative where the actual classification is "attack" but the

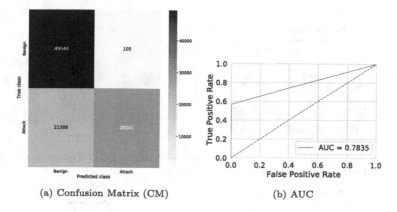

(a) Confusion Matrix (CM)   (b) AUC

Fig. 3. FedSGD (supervised) with learning rate = 0.0001, epochs = 200

predicted classification is "benign". The diagonal values represent the accuracy of the model [11]. 3) Area Under Curve (AUC) is used with respect to binary classification problems. The probability that a randomly chosen positive record will be ranked higher than the negative record is indicated by the AUC. To plot this, false positive rate and true positive rate are used. Greater values represent a better-performing model. 4) The F1 score measures the accuracy of the test. It is the preciseness and robustness of a model. As with AUC, the higher the F1 score, the better the performance of the model [11].

4.1 Federated Supervised Learning

For federated supervised learning, we train each client on local epochs and then send the model parameters to the global model for averaging. In our experiments, we use 10 clients, and each client has trained locally over 10 epochs. The parameters averaged for the global model vary based on the algorithms. Some train clients around epochs and use communication rounds for model averaging, while other algorithms train clients on a single epoch, so the model takes place in multiple periods on average and does not use rounds. We discuss these details with the results of every algorithm in the following sections.

FedSGD. In the FedSGD Algorithm, the local clients are trained on a single epoch and the gradient averaging is done after each epoch at the global model. At the client level, we define parameters such as learning rate and batch size. For FedSGD, the batch size is the number of records on each client. We conducted a total of 6 experiments to evaluate the performance of the model using three learning rates - 0.001, 0.0001, 0.00001, and in each experiment, we trained the models using 100 and 200 epochs - 10 rounds per epoch for 10 epochs and 20 rounds per epoch for 10 epochs - to compare with other algorithms. The highest accuracy of 78% is obtained for the model trained with a learning rate of 0.0001 and Epochs = 200. We use Pytorch SGD [12] optimizer and BCEWithLogitsLoss

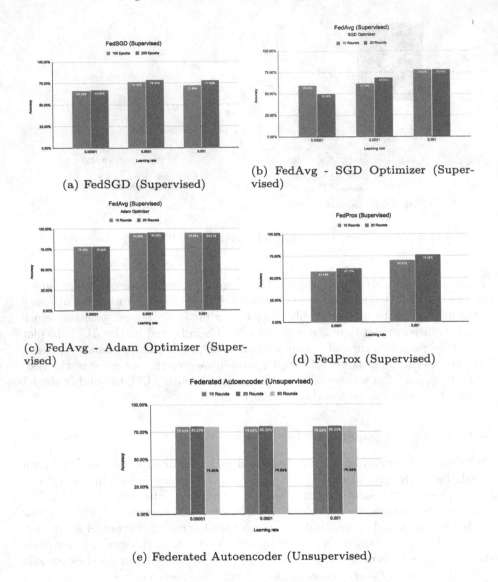

(a) FedSGD (Supervised)

(b) FedAvg - SGD Optimizer (Supervised)

(c) FedAvg - Adam Optimizer (Supervised)

(d) FedProx (Supervised)

(e) Federated Autoencoder (Unsupervised)

Fig. 4. Accuracy of different federated learning algorithms

[13] to calculate the loss. The result of this model is shown in Fig. 3. According to Fig. 3a, the model has a high false negative and classified a large number of attack records as benign. The AUC plot in Fig. 3b has a value of 0.78.

In Fig. 4a, we analyze the performance of the model by changing the learning rate and the number of epochs. We learn that the highest accuracy of 78% is achieved for 200 Epochs with a learning rate of 0.0001. For a learning rate of 0.00001, the model does not perform as well as that for other learning rates. We can also see that the number of epochs affects the accuracy of the learning

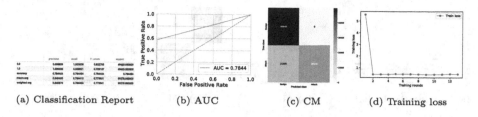

(a) Classification Report   (b) AUC   (c) CM   (d) Training loss

Fig. 5. FedAvg SGD Optimizer (Supervised) with learning rate = 0.001, epochs = 10, rounds = 20

rate 0.0001 and 0.0001. We can conclude based on the results that the greater number of epochs results in better accuracy.

FedAvg. In the FedAvg Algorithm, the local clients are trained on epochs and the global model is averaged across rounds. Each client is trained over 10 epochs. In our experiments, we use different optimizers with the FedAvg algorithm to compare the performance. We perform 6 experiments each with SGD and Adam optimizer separately. We evaluate the performance of the model using three learning rates - 0.001, 0.0001, 0.00001. We observe that the highest accuracy of 95% is obtained for the model trained with a learning rate of 0.0001, Rounds 20 using the Adam optimizer.

The results of these models are described in Fig. 5 and Fig. 6. For the results of the FedAvg-SGD Optimizer, in Fig. 5a, the classification report shows that the accuracy rate is 78%, while the AUC value of Fig. 5b is 0.7844, which is similar to FedSGD. The training loss in Fig. 5d is for a single client. It can be seen to decrease after the first round of model averaging, and it remains stable after increasing rounds. Based on the confusion matrix, we do not see a significant difference between FedSGD and FedAvg-SGD results in terms of accuracy and classification, but a higher number of benign records are correctly classified in this case.

Figure 6 shows the results obtained using the Adam optimizer for model training and the FedAvg averaging algorithm. FedAvg is different from FedSGD in that FedSGD compares the local model with the model gradient. Compared to previous results, we see a significant increase in model accuracy, and the overall model performance also improves. In Fig. 6a, the classification report shows that the F1 scores for both attack and benign records are good. Similarly, the confusion matrix in Fig. 6c has higher true positive and true negative values. The AUC value of 0.9535 in Fig. 6b indicates that our model has a high probability of correctly classifying attack and benign data. The results show that FedAvg using Adam Optimizer is a better performing model.

Figure 4b shows that when the SGD optimizer is used with FedAvg, the highest accuracy of 78% is achieved for a learning rate of 0.001 with model-averaged for 20 rounds. The accuracy rate varies with the learning rate and global model averaging rounds. These results are comparable to FedSGD, and we see that the accuracy increases as the learning rate and rounds increase. The

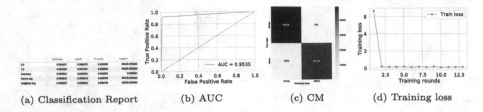

| (a) Classification Report | (b) AUC | (c) CM | (d) Training loss |

Fig. 6. FedAvg Adam Optimizer (Supervised) with learning rate = 0.001, epochs = 10, rounds = 20

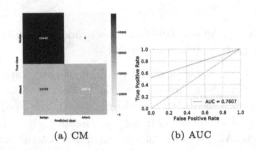

| (a) CM | (b) AUC |

Fig. 7. FedProx (supervised) with learning rate = 0.001, epochs = 20, rounds = 10

model does not perform well with for learning rate of 0.00001. In the case of FedSGD the global model is averaged after every epoch in the client while in the case of FedAvg, the model averaging occurs after several epochs on each client. In our case, we fix the number of epochs on each client as 10.

In Fig. 4c, we observe a huge improvement in accuracy compared to other models. Contrasted with SGD, the FedAvg algorithm uses the Adam optimizer to perform better, with the same learning rate, and an average of 0.001 for 20 rounds. The highest accuracy rate is 95%, which is also the highest accuracy rate obtained by the supervised learning model in the federated framework. We see that the choice of optimizer during model training makes a difference in the performance of the model. Even in the case when Adam optimizer is used, the model accuracy is 78.30% for a learning rate of 0.00001 for both 10, 20 rounds. The number of rounds over which the global model is averaged does not affect the model accuracy significantly. Therefore, we can conclude that the choice of optimizer and learning rate mainly determines the model performance of a supervised DNN trained using federated learning and a global model aggregated using the FedAvg algorithm.

FedProx. The FedProx algorithm uses a similar implementation as FedSGD and FedAvg but uses an extra parameter μ, a variable parameter similar to learning rate. We train the model using three learning rates - 0.001, 0.0001, 0.00001, and each experiment used 10 and 20 rounds for training. Each client uses 10 epochs for training locally. We perform a total of 12 experiments for FedProx to first learn that the learning rate of 0.001 yields the highest accuracy for FedProx.

Therefore, we perform additional experiments to understand how μ affects the algorithm's performance. We use a μ of 0, 0.5, 0.9. The results below are for μ of 0.5 which indicates equal number of clients have 10 epochs and others are trained over random number of epochs less than total number of epochs.

The results for FedProx are described in Fig. 7. Figure 7a shows that the confusion matrix results are similar to that of FedAvg-SGD optimizer. We know that FedAvg and FedProx algorithms are driven by a similar model averaging logic but the difference is the number of clients that participate in each round. For model training using SGD Optimizer, we see a similar result. In the case of FedProx, the additional complexities are associated with a customized optimizer that uses additional parameters based on the clients. Clients in FedProx are trained in a variable number of epochs. Figure 7b shows the AUC value of 0.7607. This is similar to the FedAvg algorithm using SGD Optimizer.

As shown in Fig. 4d, the global model achieved an accuracy of 76% with a learning rate of 0.001 in 20 rounds of training. As we have seen in the other models described earlier, the increased number of rounds improves the accuracy of the model. The accuracy rate depends on the learning rate and the number of rounds.

4.2   Federated Unsupervised Learning

We performed 9 experiments to train the unsupervised autoencoders in a federated setting with various parameters. We trained the model using three learning rates - 0.001, 0.0001, 0.00001, and each experiment used 10, 20, and 30 rounds for training. Each client uses 10 epochs for training locally. The model trained after 20 rounds, and a learning rate of 0.001 achieved the highest accuracy rate of 80%. We use Adam [14] optimizer and MSELoss [15] a function from Pytorch to calculate the loss. For model averaging, FedAvg algorithm is implemented.

Since the reconstruction loss for attack traffic is higher than that of benign traffic, we use the reconstruction loss for the classification problem. The reconstruction loss for benign and attack traffic is shown in Fig. 8. We classify the traffic as benign and attack based on a threshold value, which is calculated using the normal distribution described in the Eq. 4 below.

$$Threshold = \mu + \sigma \tag{4}$$

The result of this model is shown in Fig. 9. Figure 9c shows that for the selected threshold, the autoencoder can correctly classify a larger number of benign records than the attack records. The right value of the threshold is important for classification. If we use a higher threshold, we will see that all benign records will be correctly classified, but it will also affect the number of attack records that are misclassified. For unsupervised learning, as the model is trained on an unlabeled data set, reconstruction loss helps to calculate the threshold required for classification. We see that using Eq. 4 for determining threshold value yields better results compared to the randomly chosen value.

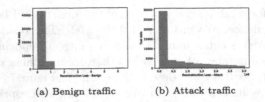

(a) Benign traffic   (b) Attack traffic

Fig. 8. Reconstruction loss for federated autoencoder (unsupervised)

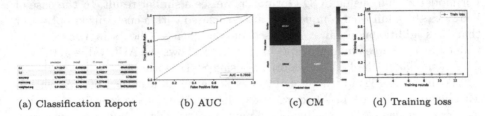

(a) Classification Report   (b) AUC   (c) CM   (d) Training loss

Fig. 9. Results - federated autoencoder (unsupervised)

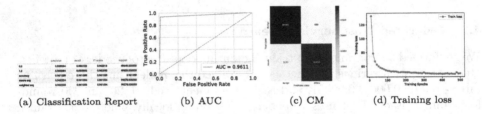

(a) Classification Report   (b) AUC   (c) CM   (d) Training loss

Fig. 10. Results - centralized DNN (supervised)

4.3   Centralized Supervised Learning

We trained a deep neural network in a centralized setting, where the DNN model is trained on the complete data set. The highest accuracy of 96% is obtained for the model trained with a learning rate of 0.0001, Epochs = 500. We use Adam [14] optimizer and MSELoss [15] from Pytorch function to calculate the loss. The result of this model is shown in Fig. 10. Overall, we see that Centralized DNN has a high classification accuracy and a high f1 score for both attack and benign labels.

4.4   Centralized Unsupervised Learning

For unsupervised learning, we train an autoencoder. The model trained with a learning rate of 0.0001 can achieve the highest accuracy rate of 80% with 500 epochs. The result of this model is shown in Fig. 11. We see that the results are similar to those of an unsupervised autoencoder trained using a federated framework. The model can classify attack and benign records with an accuracy of 80%.

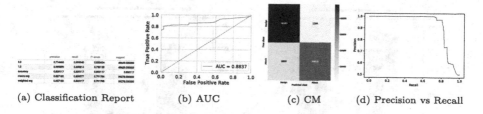

(a) Classification Report   (b) AUC   (c) CM   (d) Precision vs Recall

Fig. 11. Results - centralized autoencoder (unsupervised)

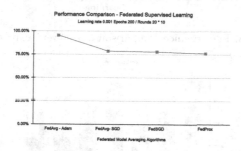

Fig. 12. Federated supervised learning-model averaging algorithms

4.5 Performance Comparison

In this section, we compare the performance of supervised and unsupervised machine learning models trained in centralized and federated frameworks.

Federated Supervised Learning - Averaging Algorithms. For federated supervised learning, we compared the performance of the global model averaging algorithm results in terms of accuracy. As shown in Fig. 12, the FedAvg algorithm using DNN trained with Adam optimizer on each client for 10 epochs and a learning rate of 0.001 for 20 rounds perform best with an accuracy of more than 95%. Among other algorithms that use the SGD optimizer, FedProx has the lowest accuracy which is close to 75%.

Federated - Supervised vs Unsupervised Learning. We compare the performance of supervised learning and unsupervised learning in the federated framework. As shown in Fig. 13a, the performance of supervised learning is better than unsupervised learning due to the labeled data that can be used for model training and evaluation. The accuracy of federated supervised DNN models is around 95% while for federated unsupervised autoencoder, the accuracy is close to 80%. For federated unsupervised autoencoder, we use the results of FedAvg-Adam experiments for global model averaging. We conclude that supervised learning performs better than unsupervised learning in a federated framework for IoT attack detection.

Unsupervised - Centralized vs Federated Learning. We compare the accuracy of unsupervised autoencoders implemented in federated and centralized frameworks. For federated unsupervised autoencoder, we use the results of

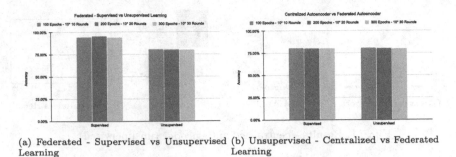

(a) Federated - Supervised vs Unsupervised Learning

(b) Unsupervised - Centralized vs Federated Learning

Fig. 13. Performance comparison of different categories

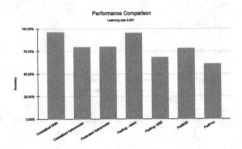

Fig. 14. Comparison - supervised, unsupervised, federated, centralized learning

FedAvg-Adam for global model averaging. As you can see from Fig. 13b, there is no significant difference between the results and the accuracy is close to 80%. Thus, for real-time analysis of unlabeled data, we can use federated learning for IoT attack detection to protect data privacy.

Comparison - Supervised, Unsupervised, Federated, Centralized Learning. We compare the accuracy of supervised and unsupervised learning in the federated and centralized frameworks in Fig. 14 and summarize our analysis as follows: 1) For supervised learning, federated and centralized frameworks achieve similar accuracy close to 95%; 2) For unsupervised learning, federated and centralized frameworks achieve similar accuracy close to 80%; 3) Among the federated averaging algorithms used for supervised learning, FedAvg using the Adam optimizer achieves the highest accuracy of 95%.

We also see a significant improvement in the accuracy of the used deep neural networks implemented in a federated framework using MQTTset. Ferrag et al. [6] achieved an accuracy of 82.60% for the federated DNN global model using IID MQTTset after 50 rounds and 10 clients. We achieve an accuracy of 95% after 20 rounds. This is faster because of the Adam Optimizer and other parameters used during model training.

As the global model is averaged using local models, the expectation is that the global model has learned about the entire network through federated learning so it should show similar results to the centralized framework. Our experiments proved that this is true and the centralized and federated frameworks result in similar accuracy. Our centralized supervised Deep Neural Network also performs better with an accuracy of 96% compared to the neural network model trained on a balanced data set in [5], where the accuracy of 90.44% is achieved. We understand that improvements in model configuration have improved our results.

We conclude that in federated and centralized frameworks, supervised DNN and unsupervised autoencoders are effective in detecting and classifying attacks in MQTTset.

5   Conclusion

In this paper, we used a public dataset called MQTTset to implement a classifier that uses deep learning to filter IoT traffic. We implemented deep learning models for supervised and unsupervised learning in a federated framework and compared their performance with a centralized implementation. For federated learning, we implemented three different types of federated averaging algorithms - FedSGD, FedAvg, and FedProx, and compared how they perform to determine, which algorithm performs better in our experimental setup. Our results showed that federated learning is effective in determining attacks in IoT traffic using deep learning models with supervised and unsupervised data.

Acknowledgement. Xiaoyan Sun and Jun Dai are supported by NSF DGE-2105801.

References

1. Gillis, A.S.: Internet of things (IoT). https://internetofthingsagenda.techtarget. com/definition/Internet-of-Things-IoT. Accessed February 2021
2. Number of internet of things (IoT) connections worldwide from 2016 to 2021, by access technology. https://www.statista.com/statistics/774002/worldwide-connected-devices-by-access-technology/. Accessed February 2021
3. Beatrice, A.: Smart home trends that will dominate 2021 and beyond, 17 January 2021. https://www.analyticsinsight.net/smart-home-trends-that-will-dominate-2021-and-beyond/. Accessed February 2021
4. Brassfield, M.: Smart devices more than doubled in US homes amid COVID pandemic, 9 June 2021. https://www.itpro.co.uk/mobile/mobile-phones/359826/smart-devices-more-than-doubled-in-us-homes-amid-covid-pandemic. Accessed October 2021
5. Vaccari, I., Chiola, G., Aiello, M., Mongelli, M., Cambiaso, E.: MQTTset, a new dataset for machine learning techniques on MQTT. Sensors **20**(22), 6578 (2020)
6. Ferrag, M.A., Friha, O., Maglaras, L., Janicke, H., Shu, L.: Federated deep learning for cyber security in the internet of things: concepts, applications, and experimental analysis. IEEE Access **9**, 138509–138542 (2021)
7. scikit-learn, Machine Learning in Python. https://scikit-learn.org/stable/. Accessed February 2021
8. McMahan, B., Moore, E., Ramage, D., Hampson, S., y Arcas, B.A.: Communication-efficient learning of deep networks from decentralized data. In: Proceedings of the 20th International Conference on Artificial Intelligence and Statistics (2017)

9. Li, T., Sahu, A.K., Zaheer, M., Sanjabi, M., Talwalkar, A., Smith, V.: Federated optimization in heterogeneous networks. arXiv preprint arXiv:1812.06127 (2018)
10. PySyft. https://github.com/OpenMined/PySyft/blob/dev/packages/syft/README.md. Accessed July 2022
11. Mishra, A.: Metrics to evaluate your machine learning algorithm, 24 February 2018. https://towardsdatascience.com/metrics-to-evaluate-your-machine-learning-algorithm-f10ba6e38234. Accessed April 2021
12. SGD. https://pytorch.org/docs/stable/generated/torch.optim.SGD.html. Accessed May 2021
13. BCEWITHLOGITSLOSS. https://pytorch.org/docs/stable/generated/torch.nn.BCEWithLogitsLoss.html. Accessed May 2021
14. TORCH.OPTIM: PyTorch. https://pytorch.org/docs/stable/optim.html. Accessed April 2021
15. MSELOSS: PyTorch. https://pytorch.org/docs/stable/generated/torch.nn.MSELoss.html. Accessed April 2021

Author Index

Printed in the United States
by Baker & Taylor Publisher Services